FILE FOLDERS

:

PAINTING IN EPHEMERA

BY
LACHLAN J MCDOUGALL

©2023

LACHLAN J MCDOUGALL

LJMCD COMMUNICATIONS

ISBN: 9798367557398

ALL RIGHTS RESERVED. NO PART OF THIS BOOK MAY BE REPRODUCED WITHOUT EXPRESS WRITTEN PERMISSION OF THE AUTHOR.

ALL IMAGES COPYRIGHT LACHLAN J MCDOUGALL

IPSWICH, QUEENSLAND, AUSTRALIA

LACHLAN.MCDOUGALL@GMAIL.COM

LACHLANJMCDOUGALL.WORDPRESS.COM

OR FIND THE ARTIST ON INSTAGRAM (@LACHLANJMCDOUGALL) FACEBOOK (LACHLAN J MCDOUGALL – AUTHOR) AND TWITTER (@AUTHORLACHLAN)

Photographic prints of the images in this book are available to purchase from artpal.com/lachlanmcdougall or by emailing lachlan.mcdougall@gmail.com with your order details

THE FILE FOLDERS ARE AN EXPERIMENT IN EPHEMERA, A GLOWING NETWORK OF ARTISTS SHARING WORK ACROSS THE GLOBE WITH NO HOPE OF REWARD. TEN FOLDERS WERE INDIVIDUALLY PAINTED USING ONLY ONE BRUSH FACTORY STYLE MASS PRODUCTION, THESE COMPLETED FOLDERS WERE THEN SENT OUT WITH A LETTER TO FRIENDS AND ACQUAINTANCES IN MY MAILING NETWORK TO DO WITH WHAT THEY WILL. THEY ARE HERE TODAY GONE TOMORROW, THESE ARE NOT MUSEUM WORKS THEY ARE PERSONAL GIFTS TO HOLD IN A DOMESTIC SETTING. THIS PARTICIPATORY AESTHETIC IS CARRIED A STEP FURTHER: EACH PANEL OF THE FOLDER IS PAINTED WITH A UNIQUE IMAGE SO THAT THE RECIPIENT IS FACED WITH A DECISION OF HOW TO DISPLAY—THE FRONT OR BACK PANEL? DO I CUT THE FOLDER IN HALF TO HIGHLIGHT THE DIFFERENT IMAGES? CERTAIN PANELS ARE ALSO SIGNED IN MULTIPLE LOCATIONS TO ALLOW THE VIEWER TO DECIDE WHERE THEIR AESTHETIC SENSIBILITIES LIE. THERE IS NO RIGHT WAY UP IN SPACE—THE PAINTING GAME IS LEFT UP TO THE VIEWER TO DECIDE.

OTHER PREOCCUPATIONS TAKE ON SIMILAR FORMS TO MY WRITING. PATTERNS EMERGE FROM CHAOS, THE RANDOM CHANCE ELEMENT SHINES THROUGH WITH MAD DASH OF PAINT SLASHING AT THE CARDBOARD. THE ISSUE OF SEQUENCING AND PARTICIPATION IS THRUST TO THE FOREFRONT AND WE ARE TASKED WITH MAKING SENSE OF THE MADNESS. SOMETIMES A KEY PHRASE WILL APPEAR IN TEXT HAUNTING THE IMAGE, IT IS UP TO THE READER TO DETERMINE THEIR MEANING.

SOME OF THE IDEAS ARE BORROWED FROM WILLIAM BURROUGHS, BUT MY INTENTIONS ARE IN MANY WAYS DIFFERENT. I DO NOT INTEND TO SIMPLY JAM COMMUNICATION LINES—I INTEND TO REOPEN THEM ON A DIFFERENT PLAIN. THE FILE FOLDERS ARE AN EXPERIMENT IN DIRECT ARTISTIC COMMUNICATION. HOW SUCCESSFUL THIS TURNS OUT TO BE REMAINS TO BE SEEN.

THE ORIGINAL FOLDERS ARE ALREADY OUT IN THE WORLD LIVING THEIR BEST LIVES, BUT SCANS OF EACH PANEL HAVE BEEN MADE AVAILABLE IN PRINT. A LIMITED SIGNED A NUMBERED EDITION OF TEN PRINTS FOR EACH PANEL IS AVAILABLE WITH AN UNSIGNED 'PRINT ON DEMAND' OPTION ALSO AVAILABLE

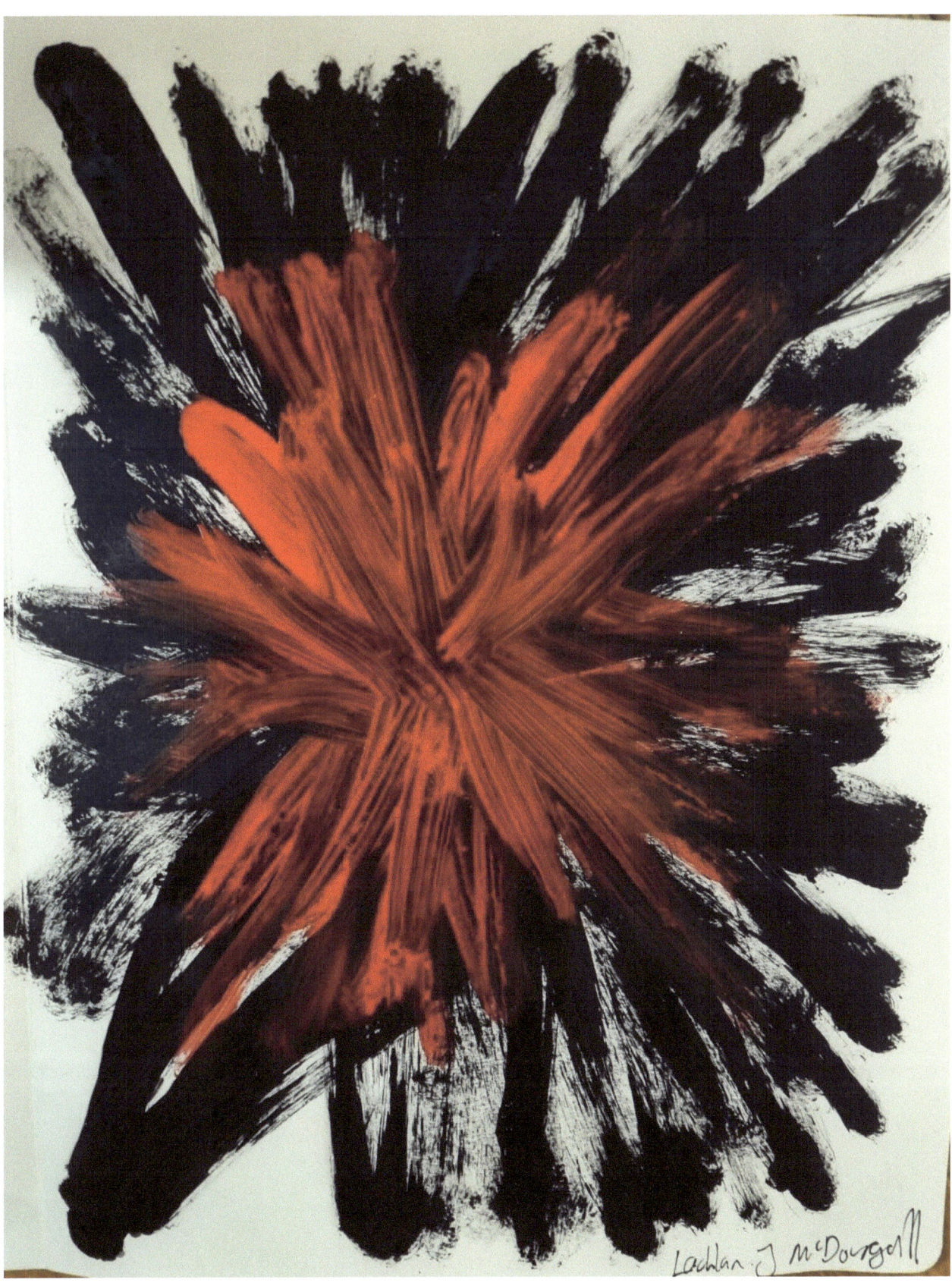

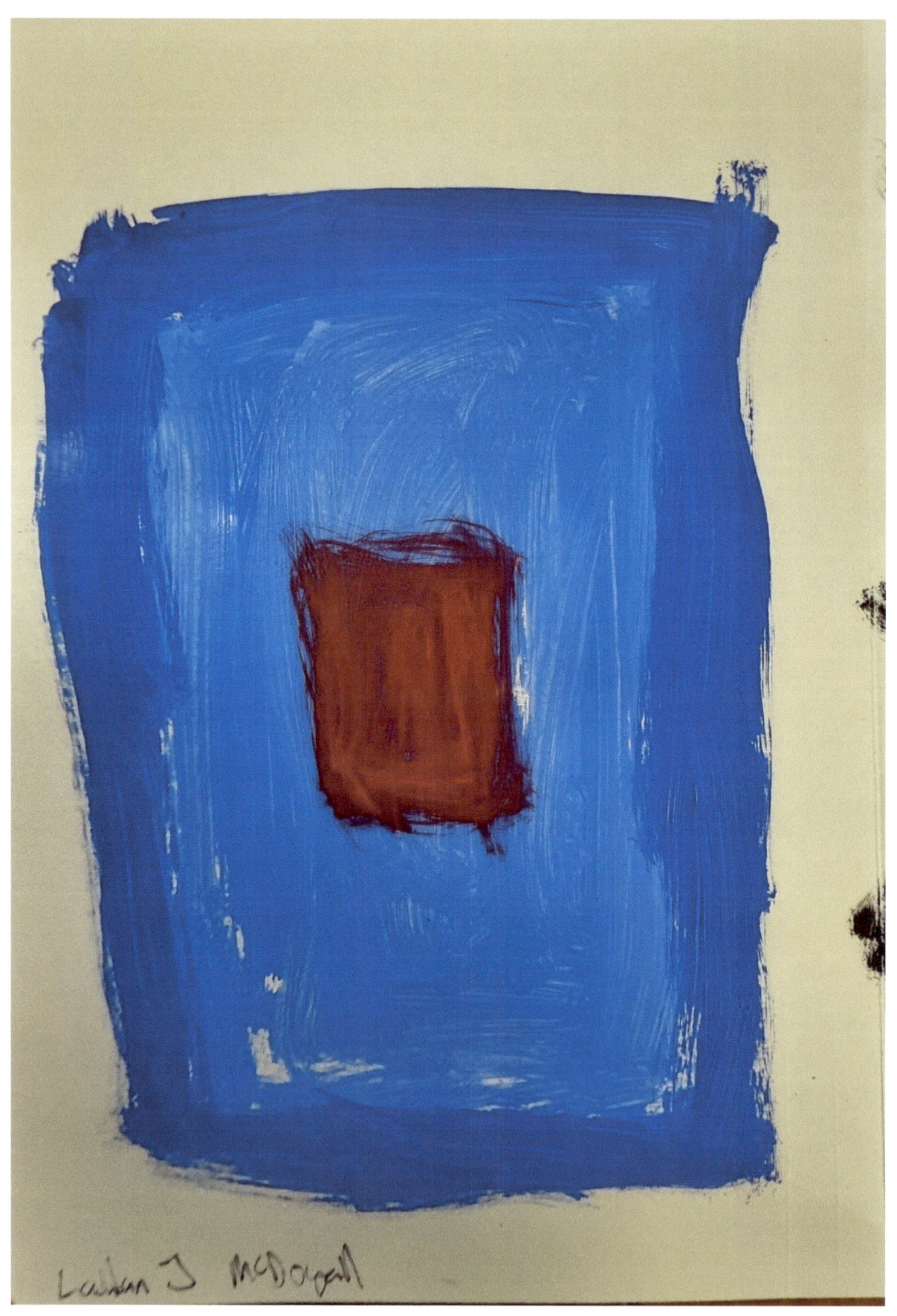

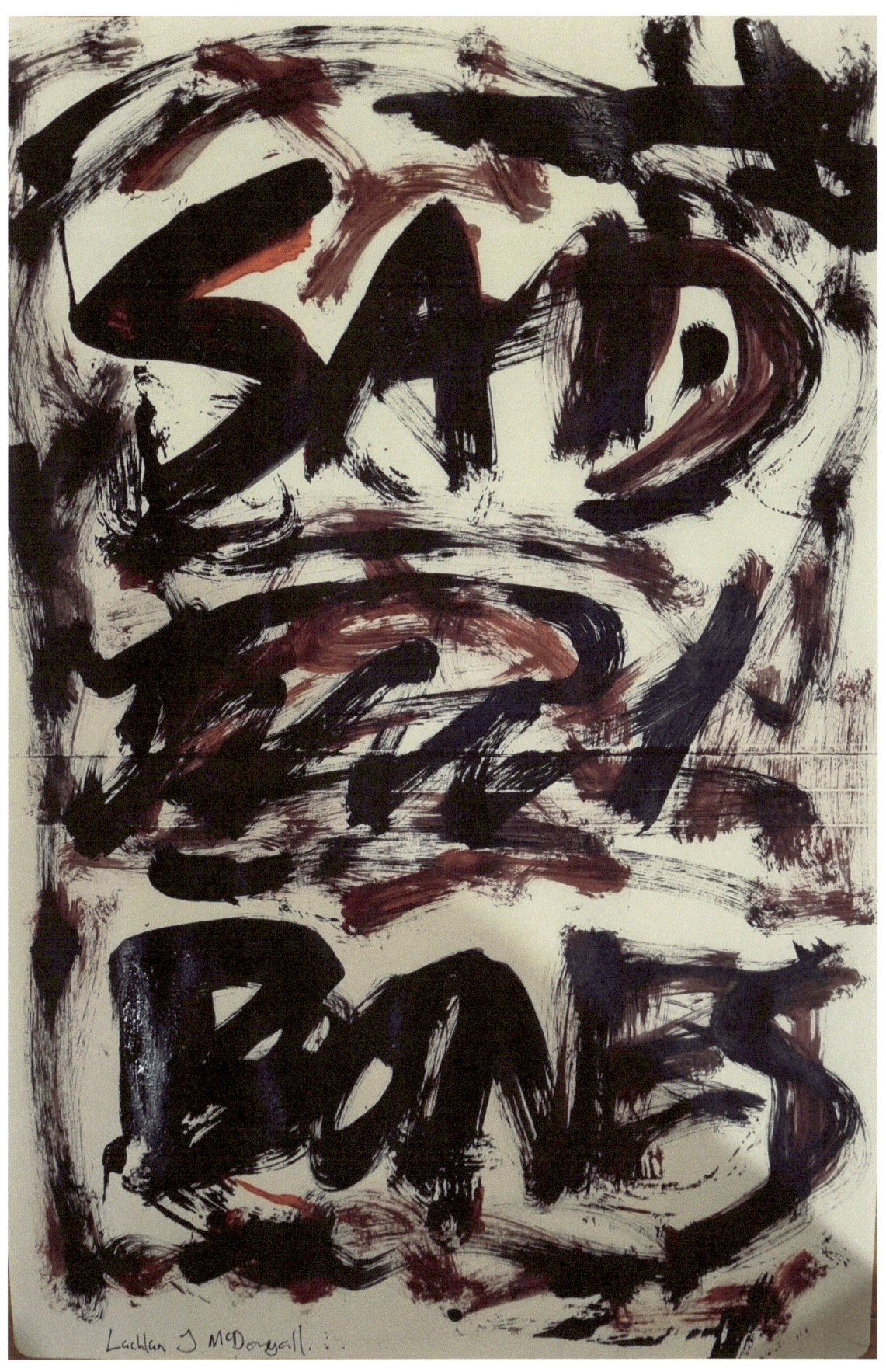

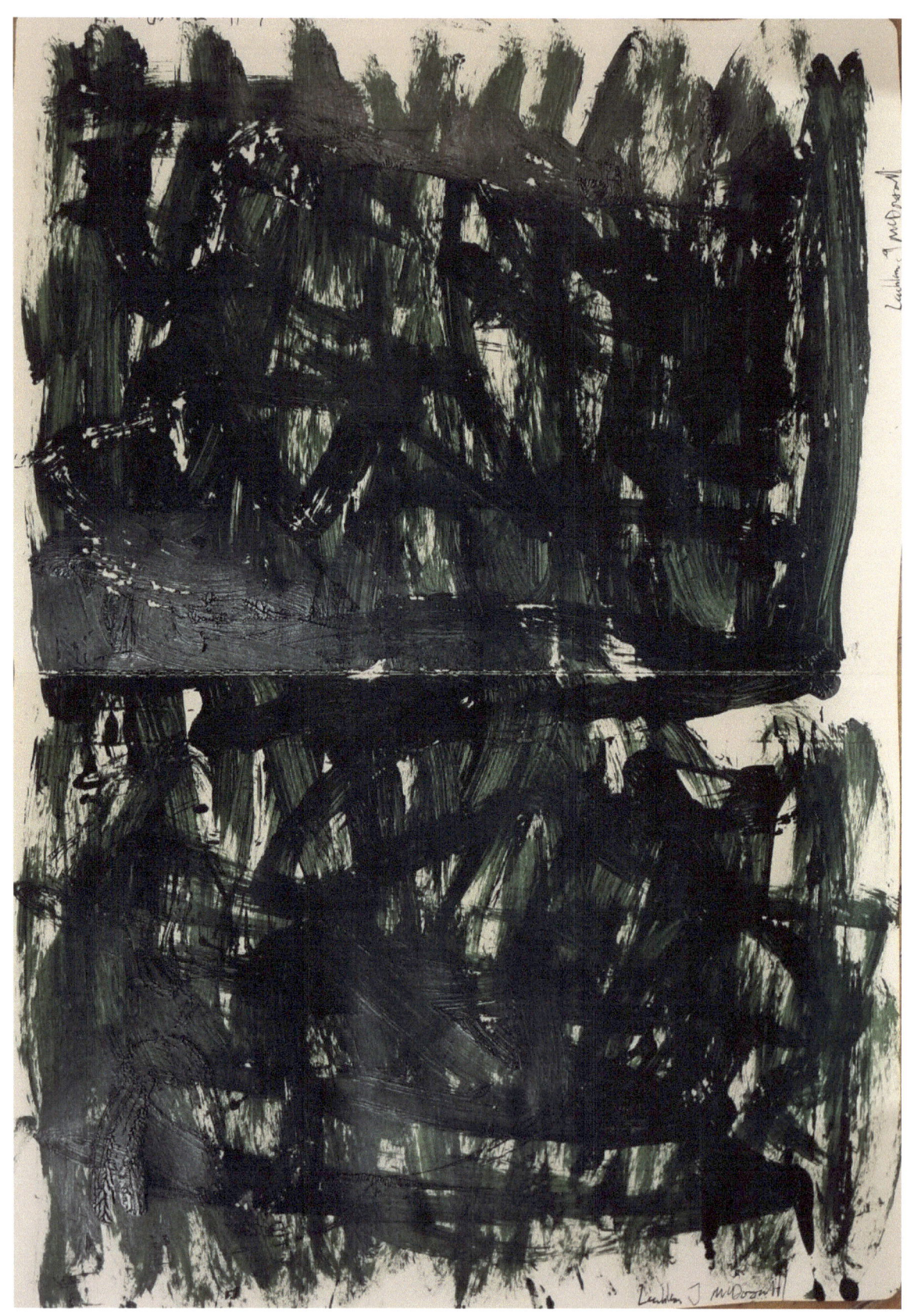

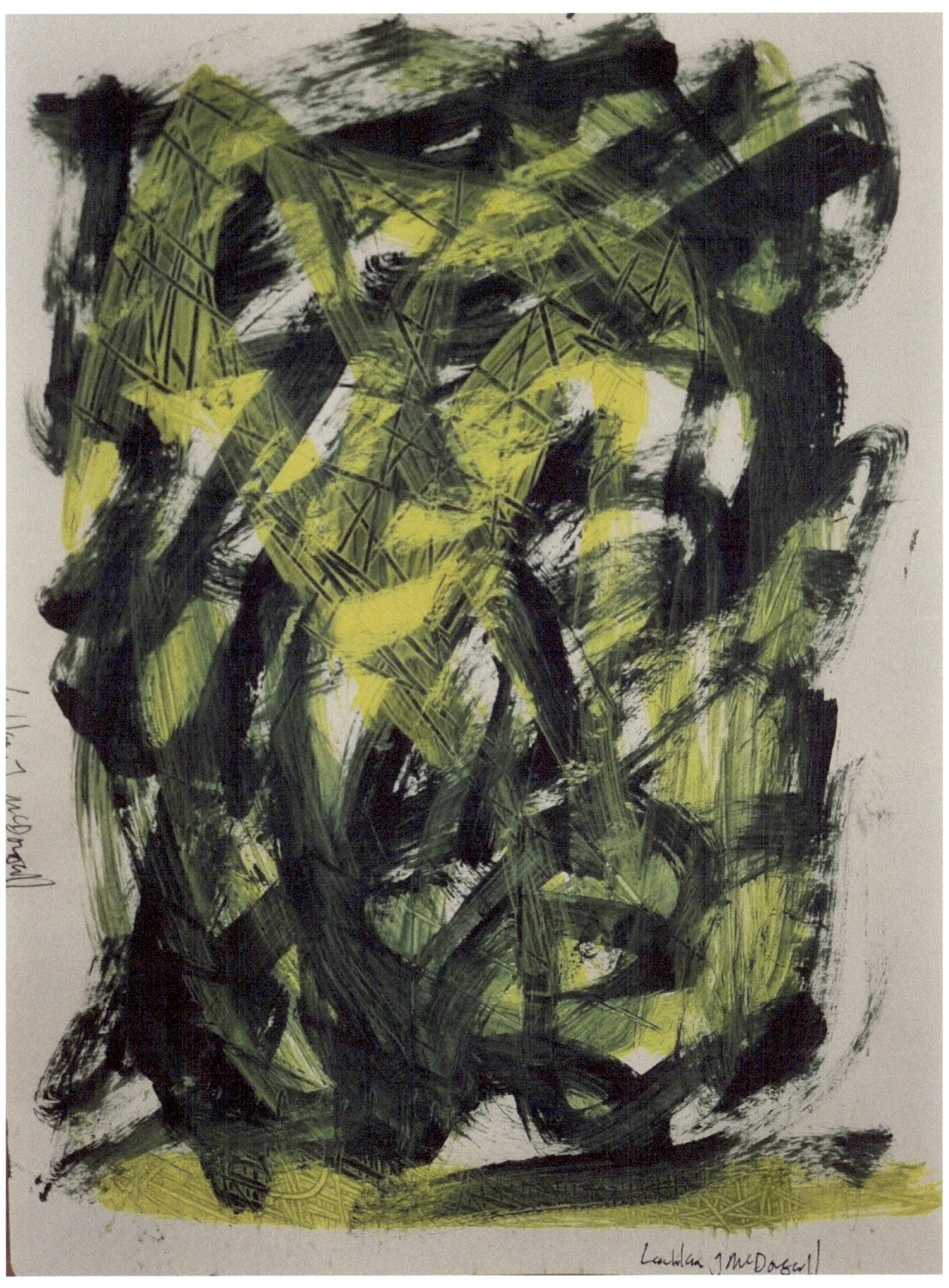

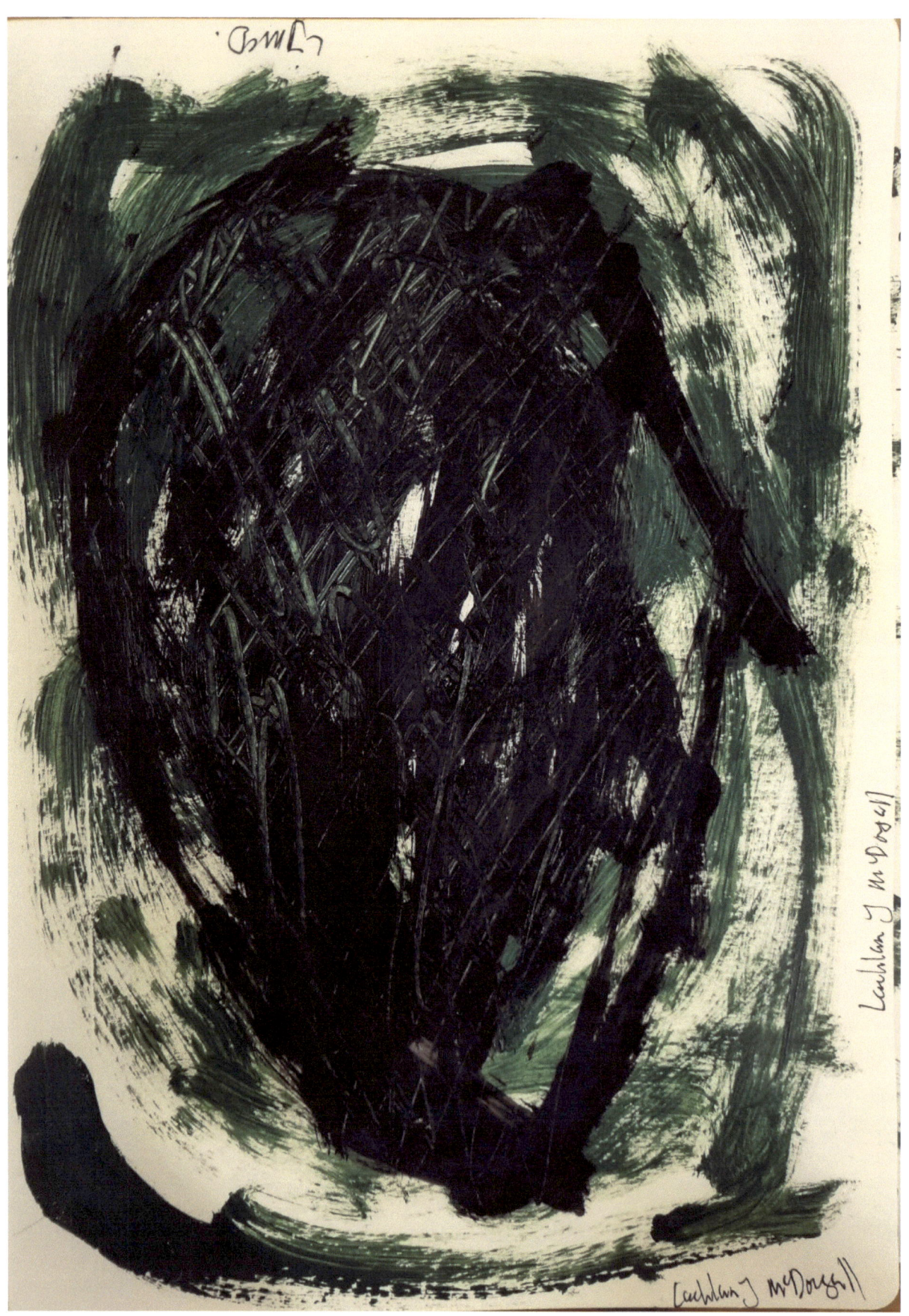

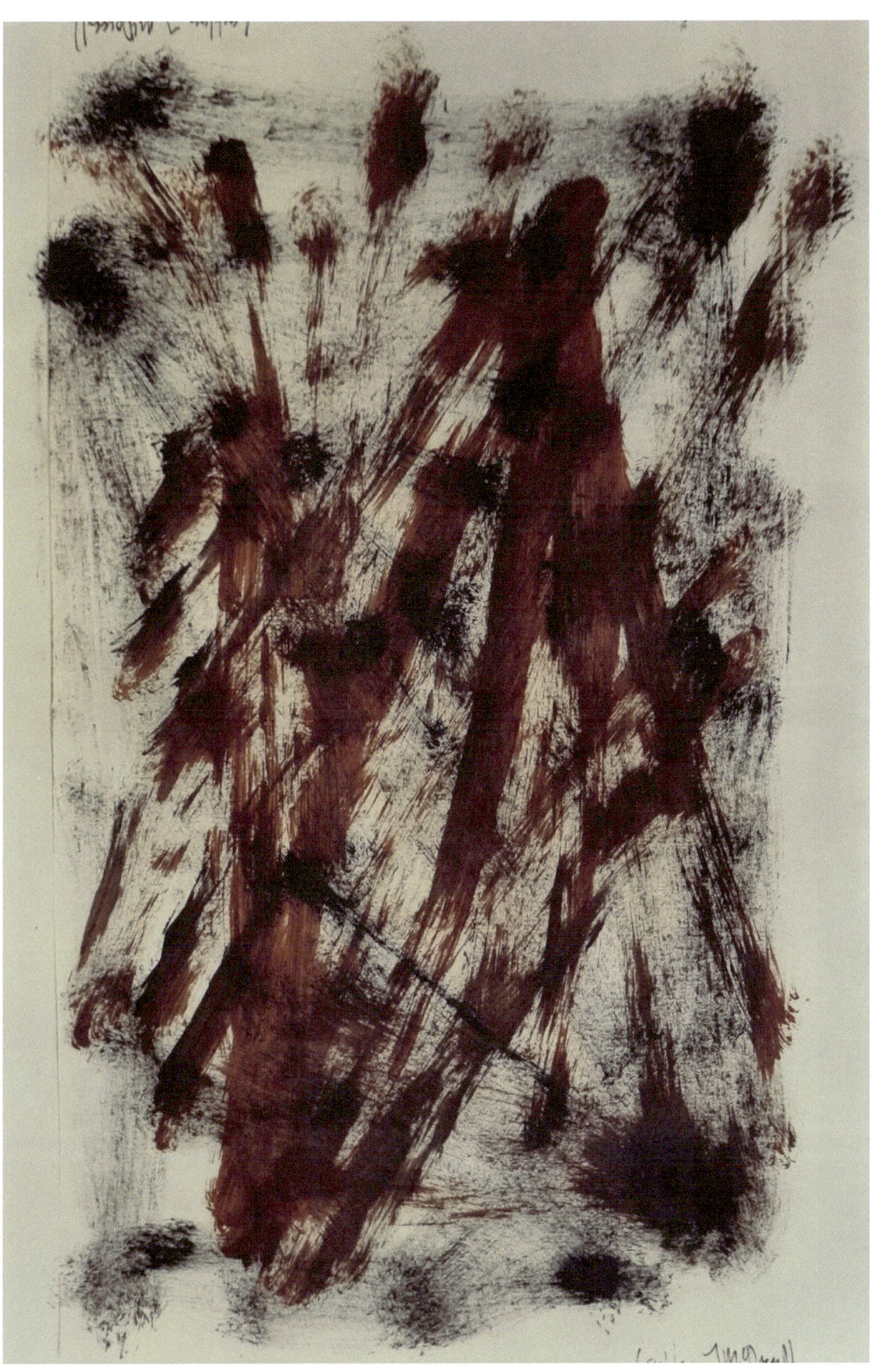

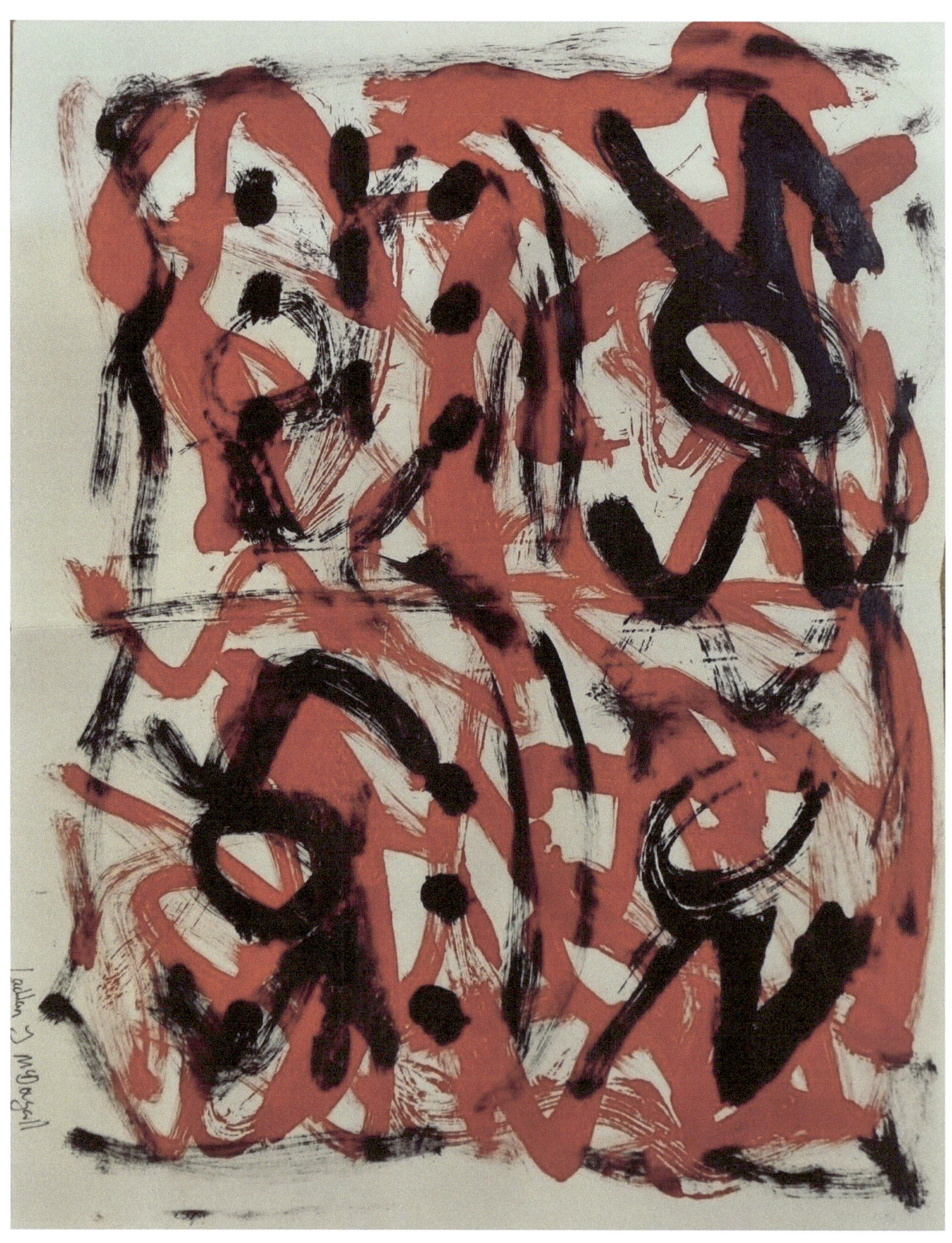

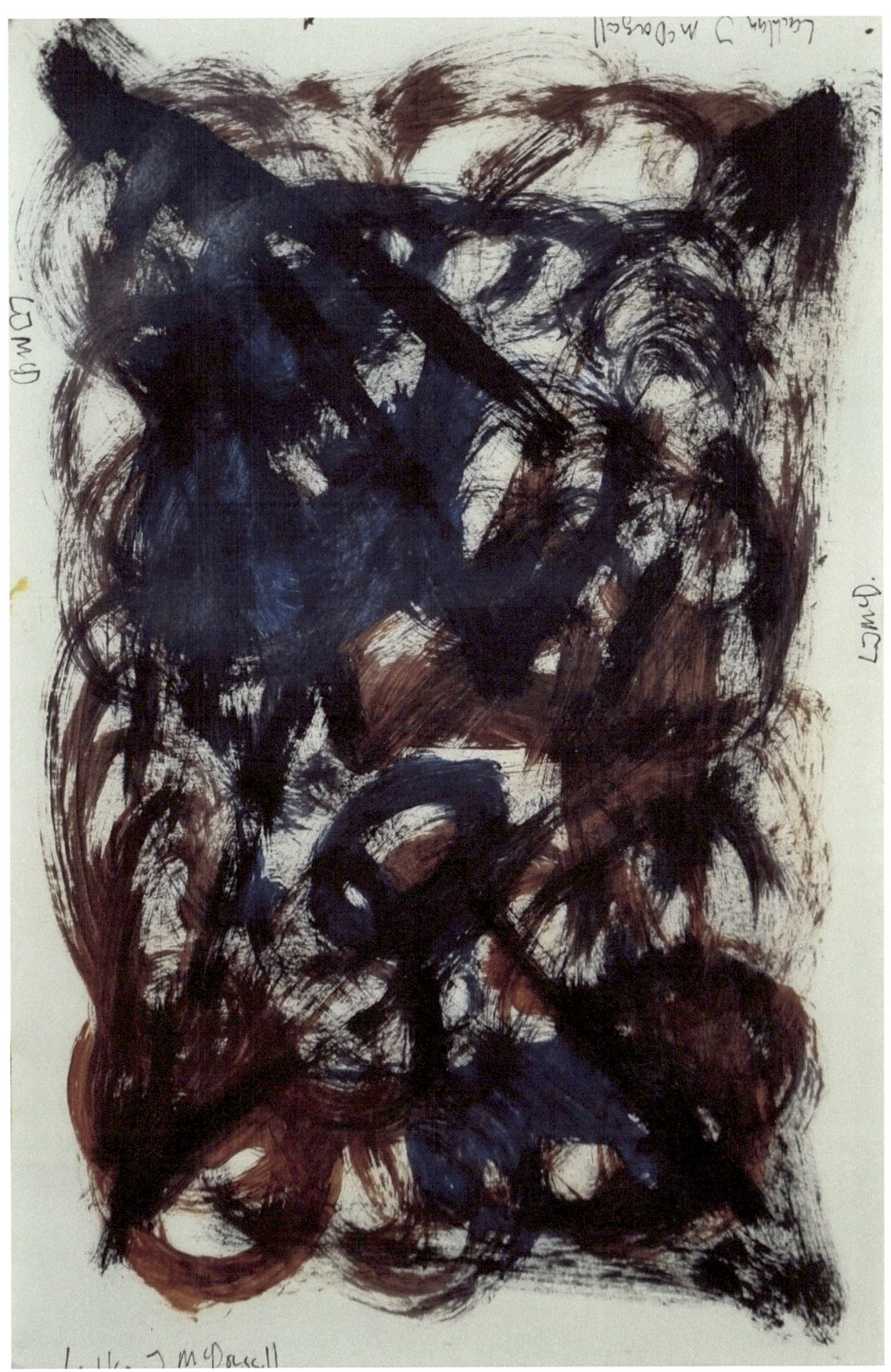

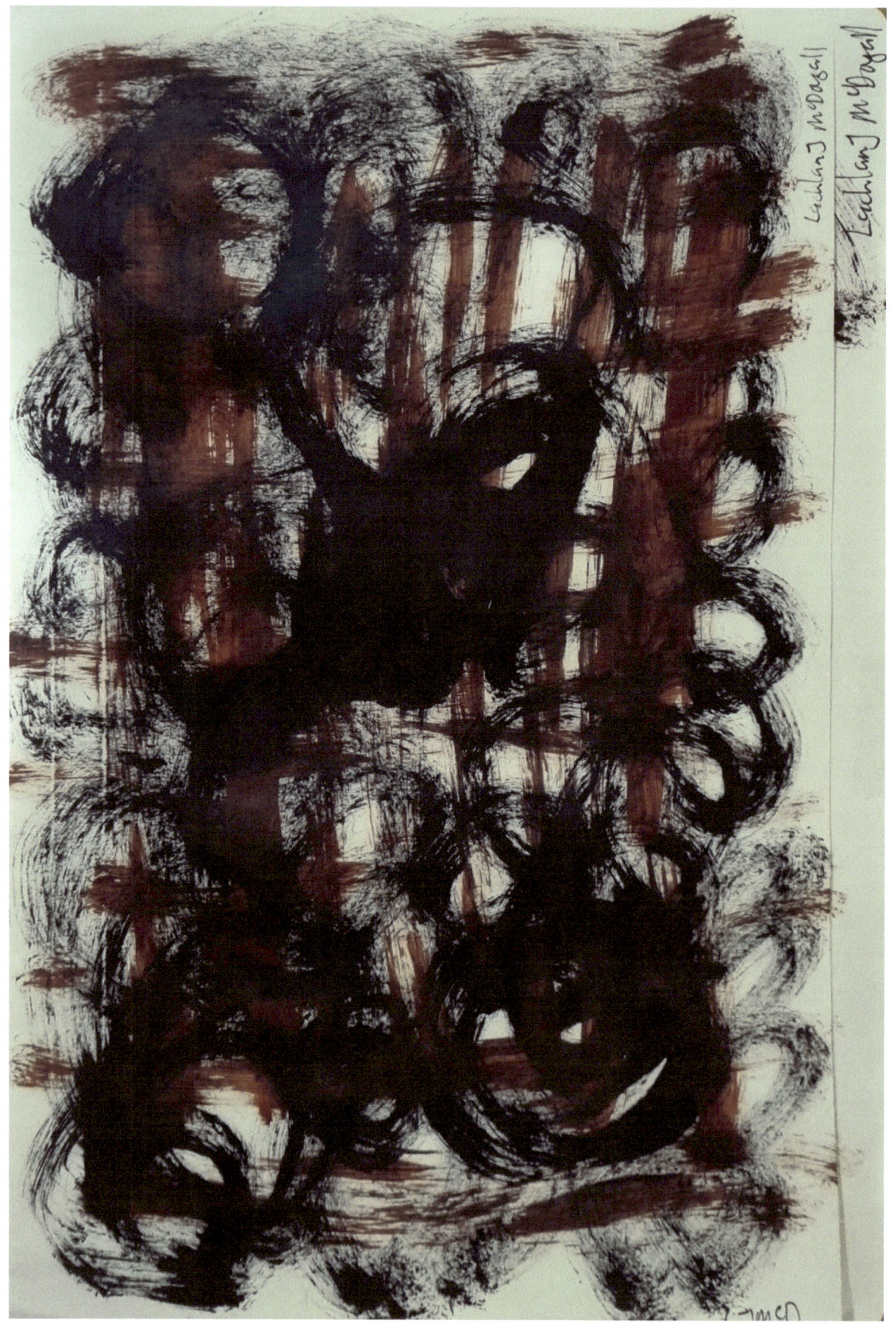

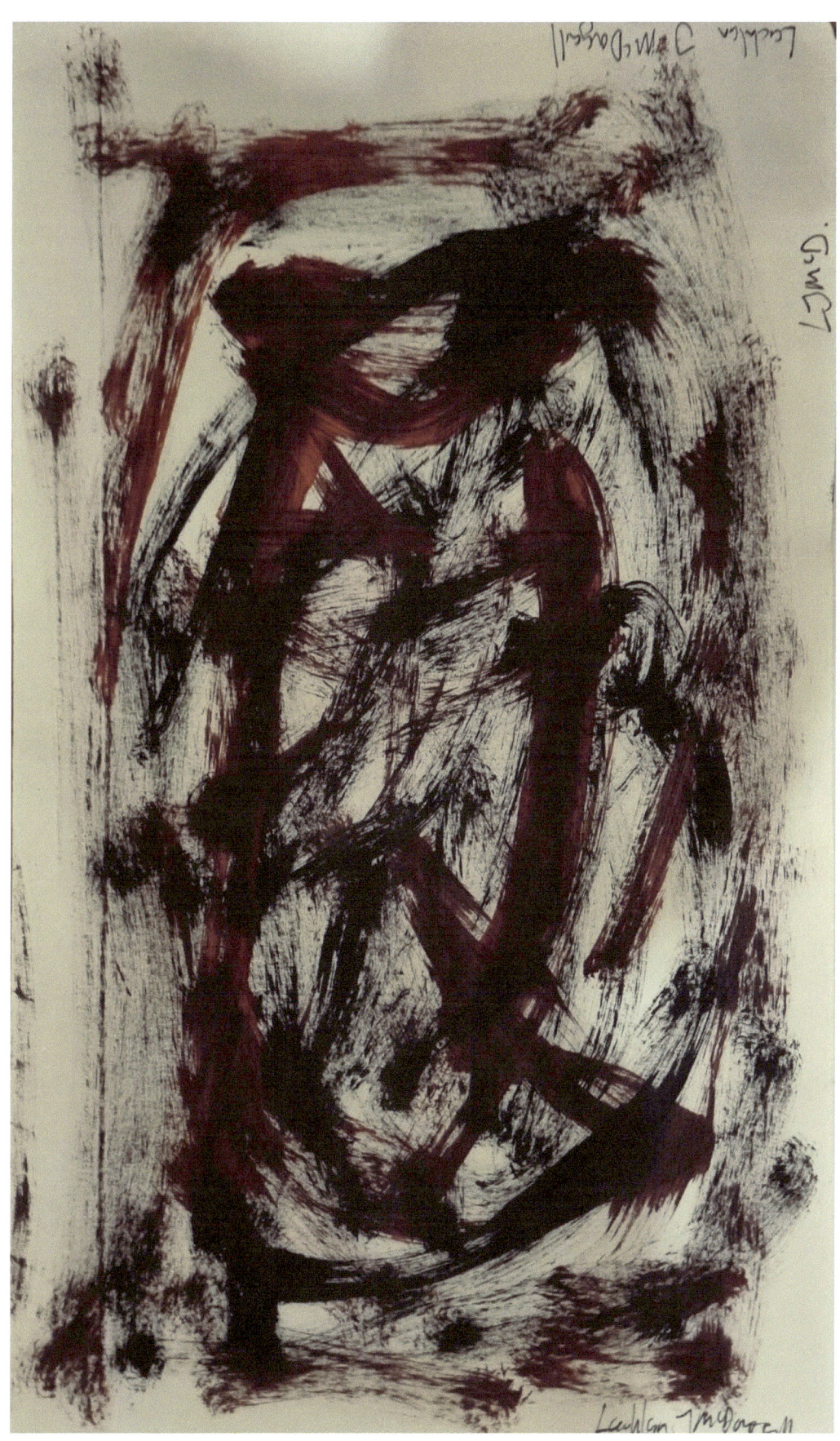

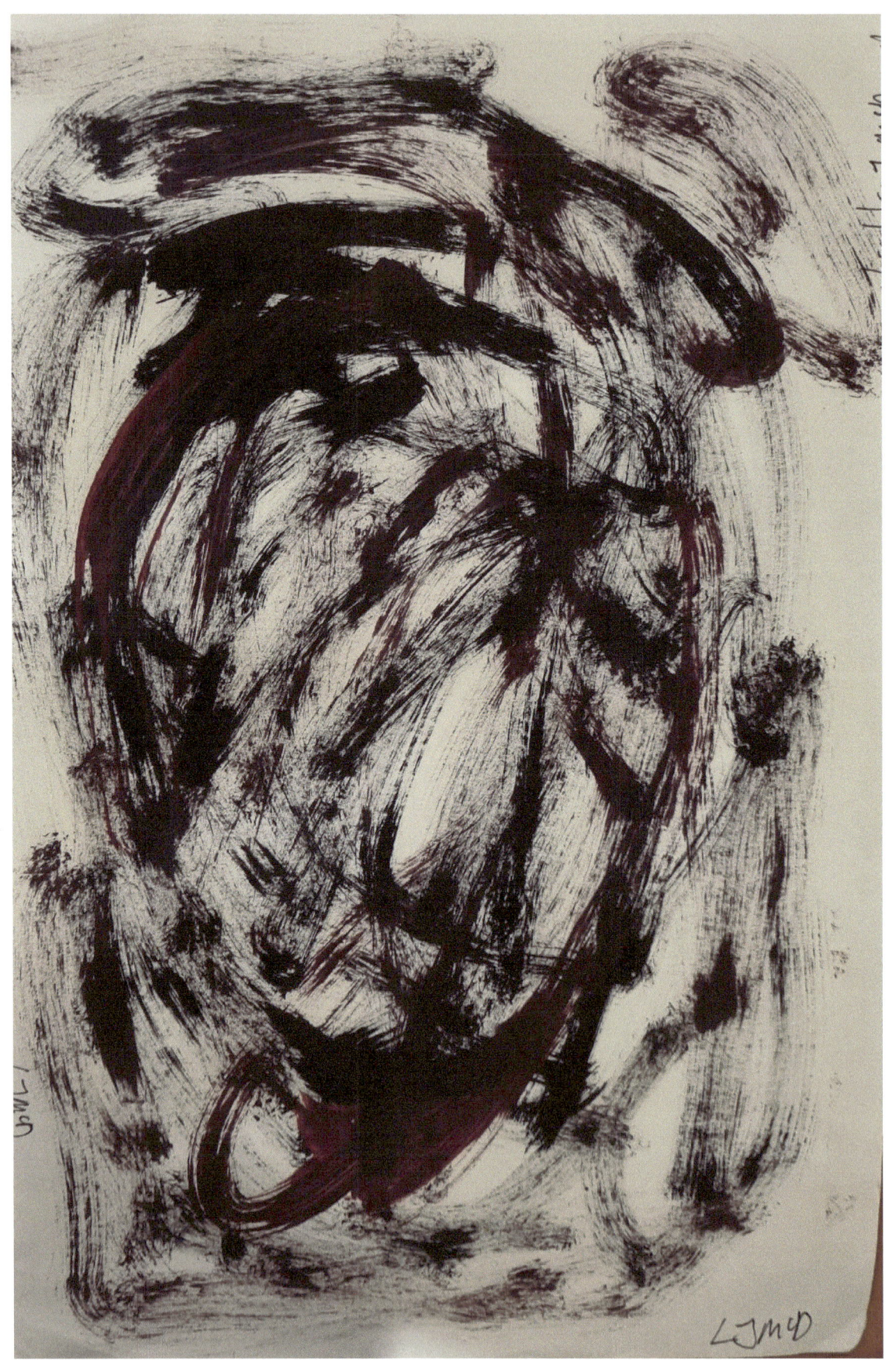

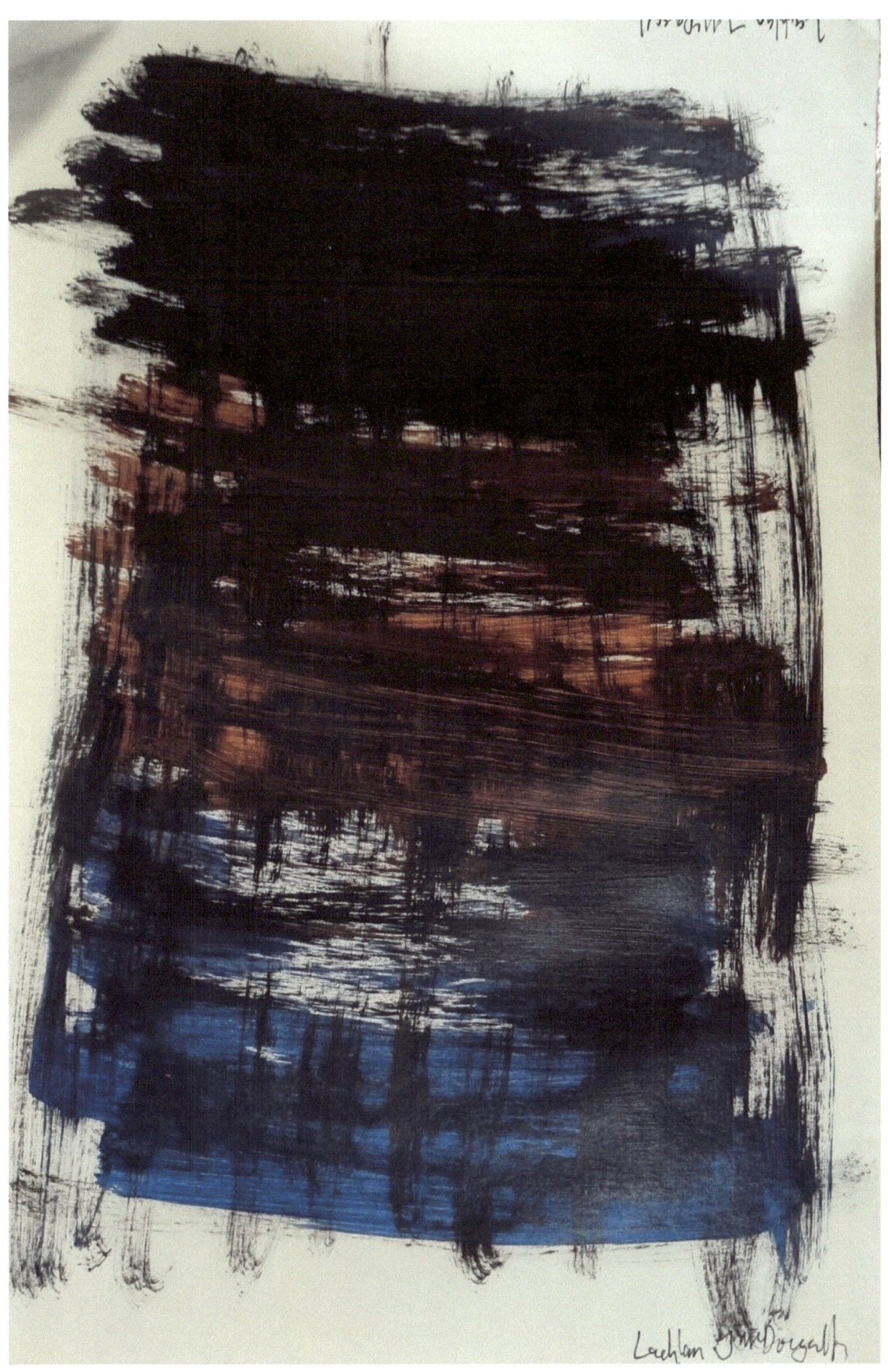

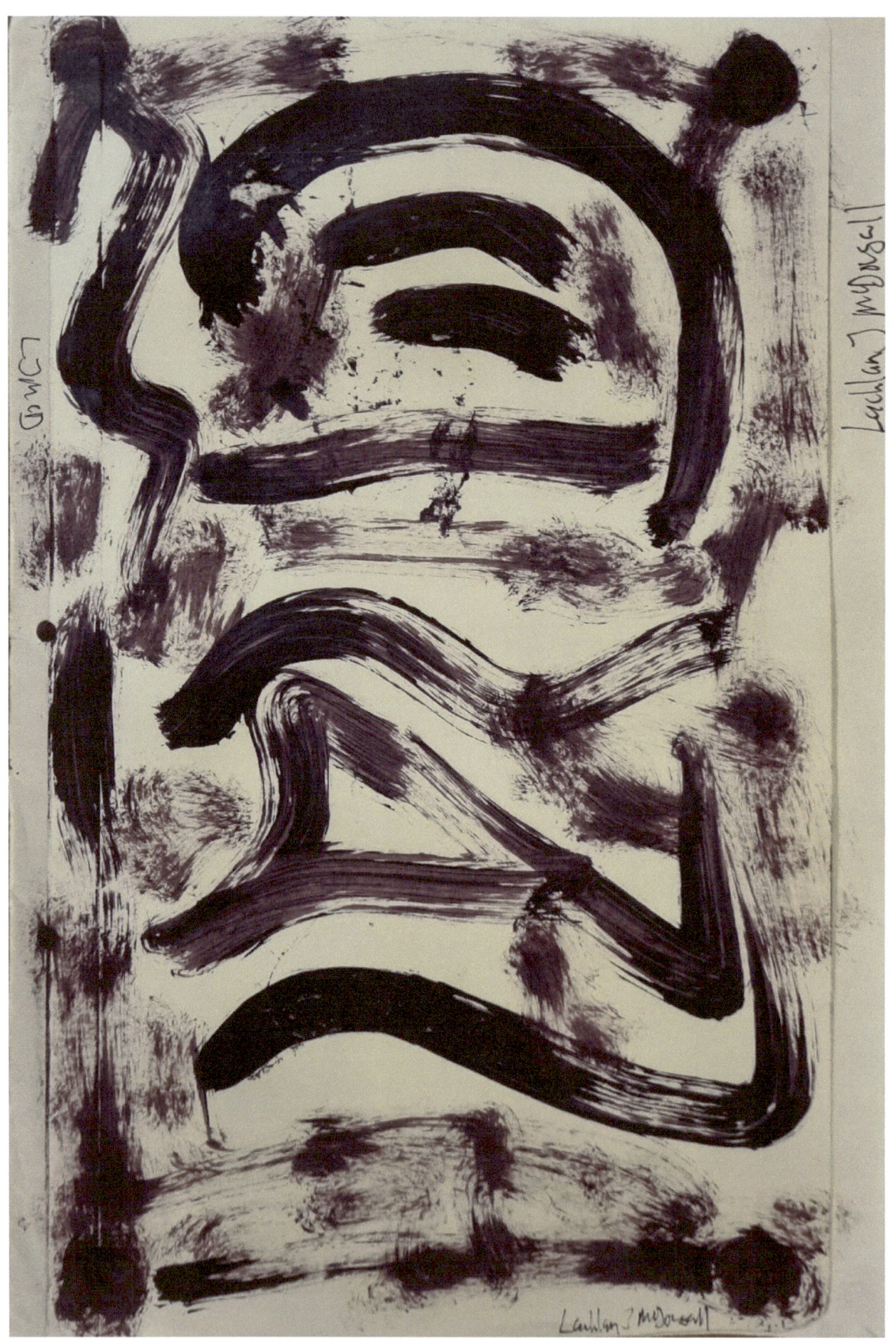

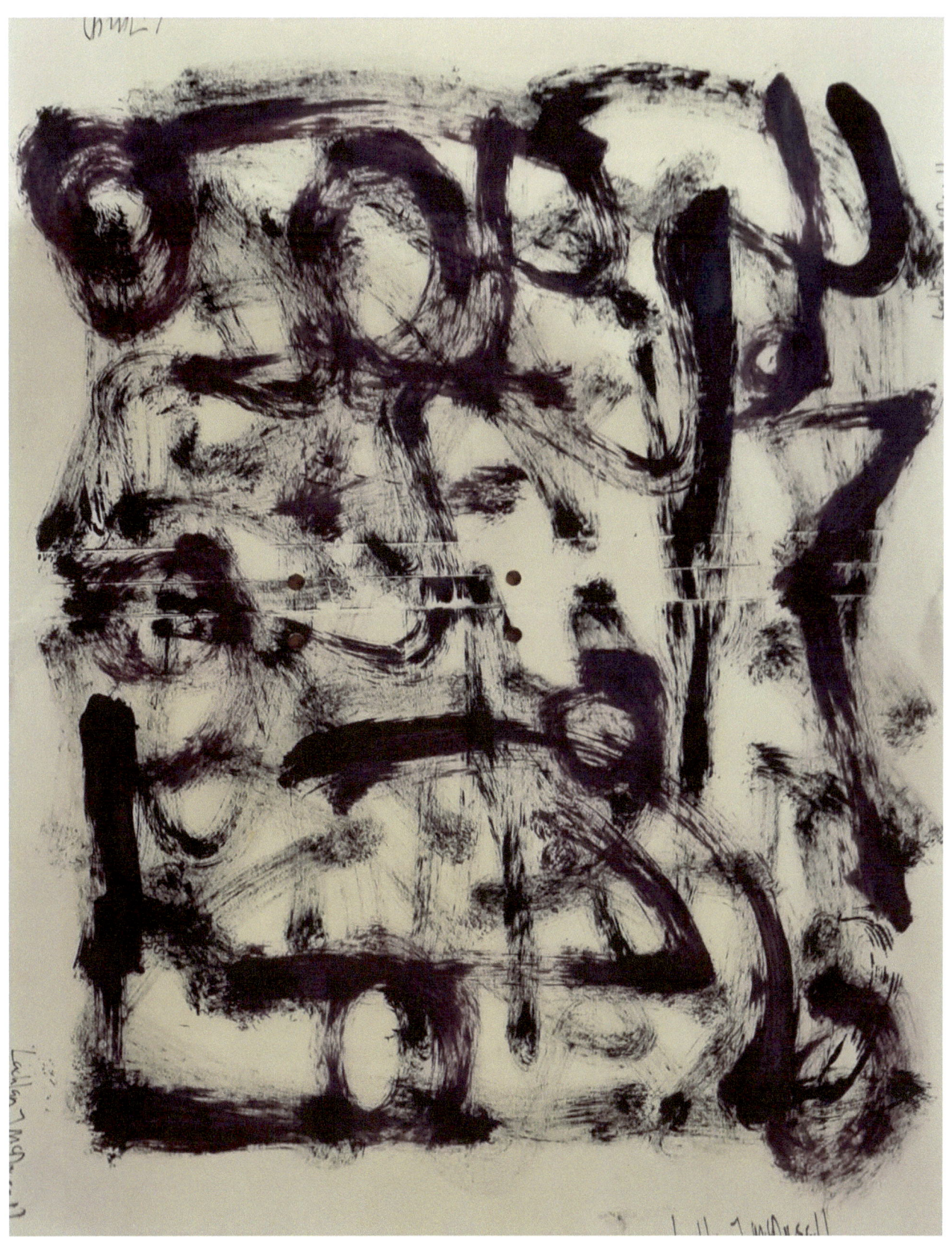

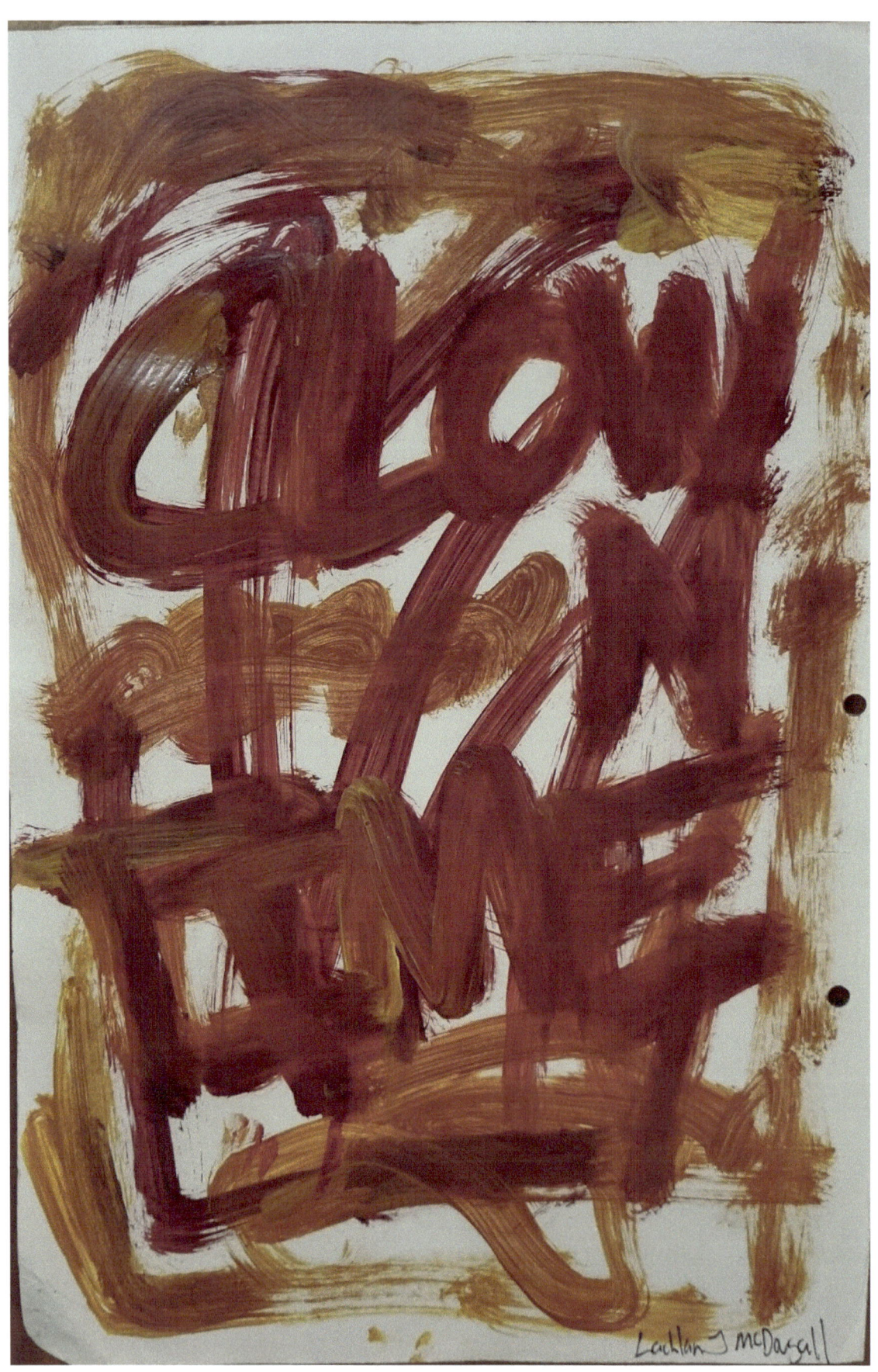

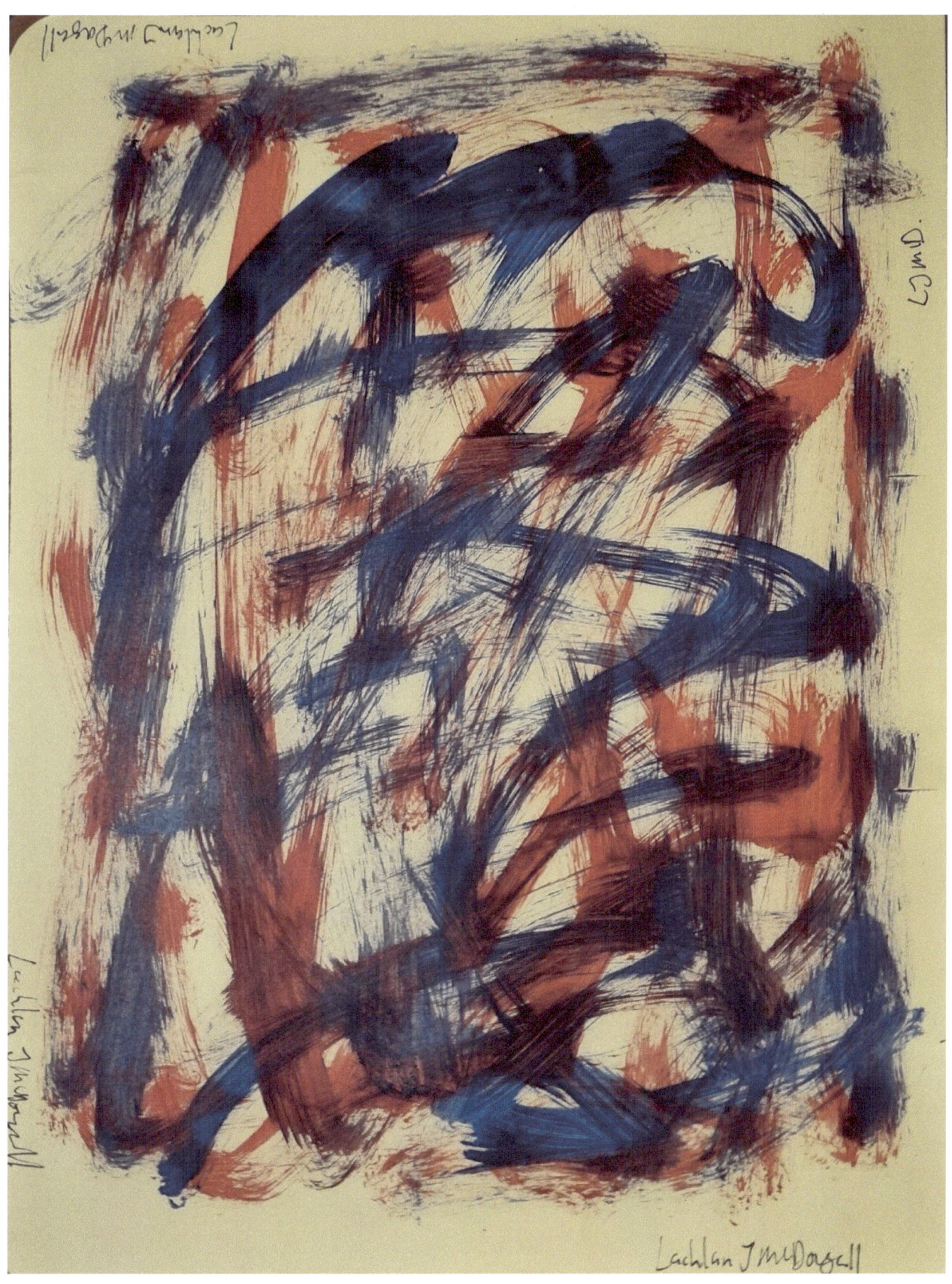

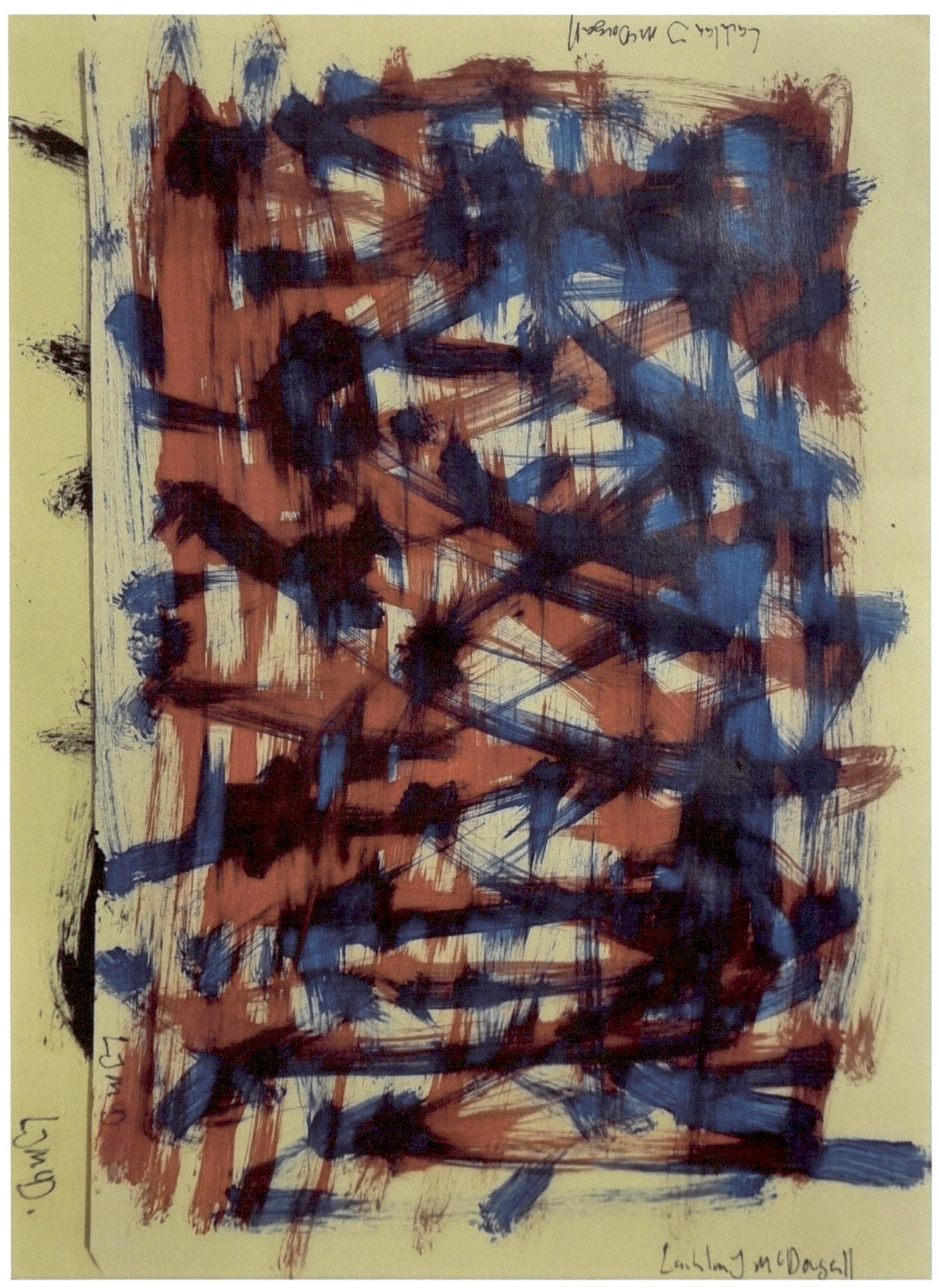

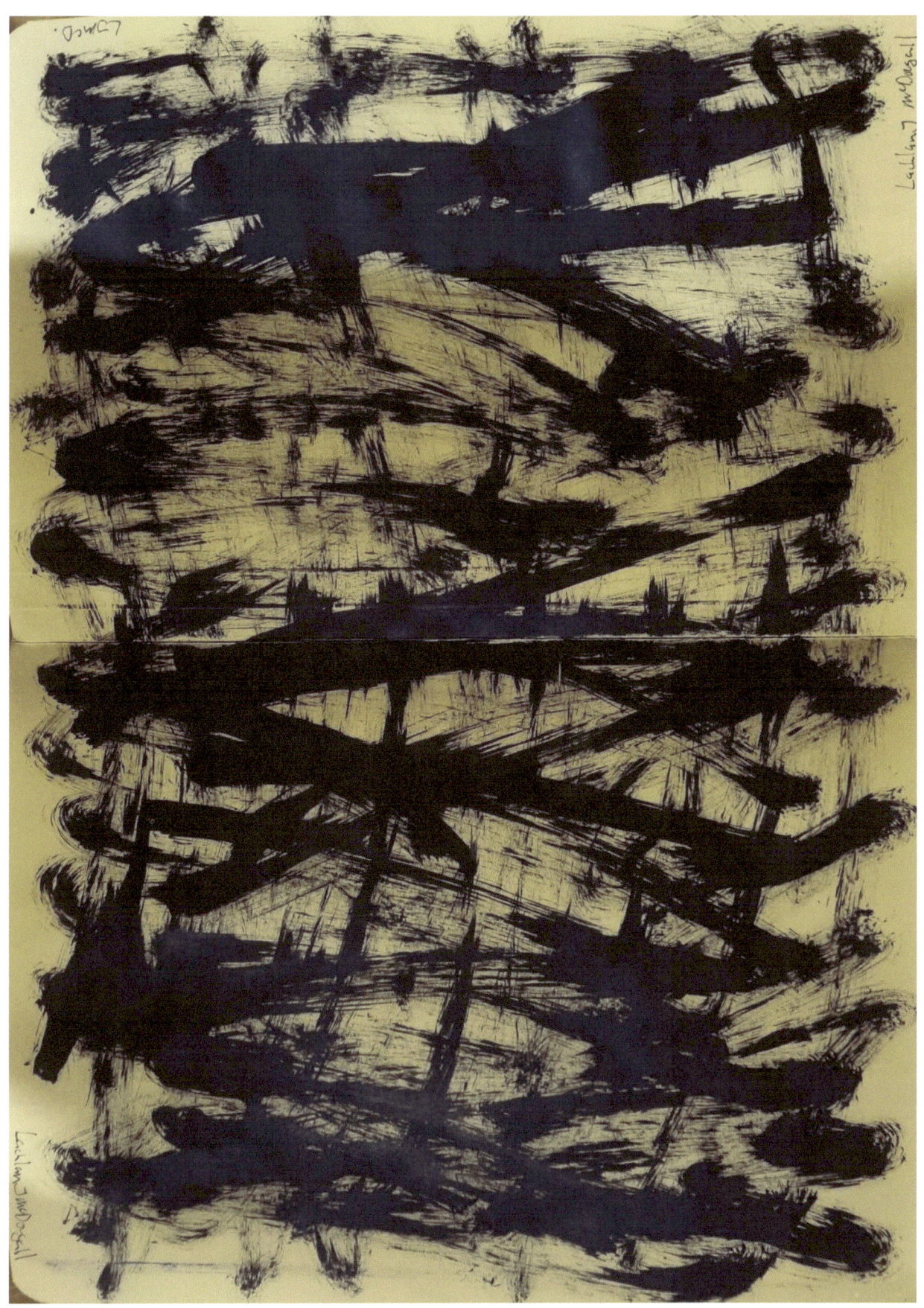

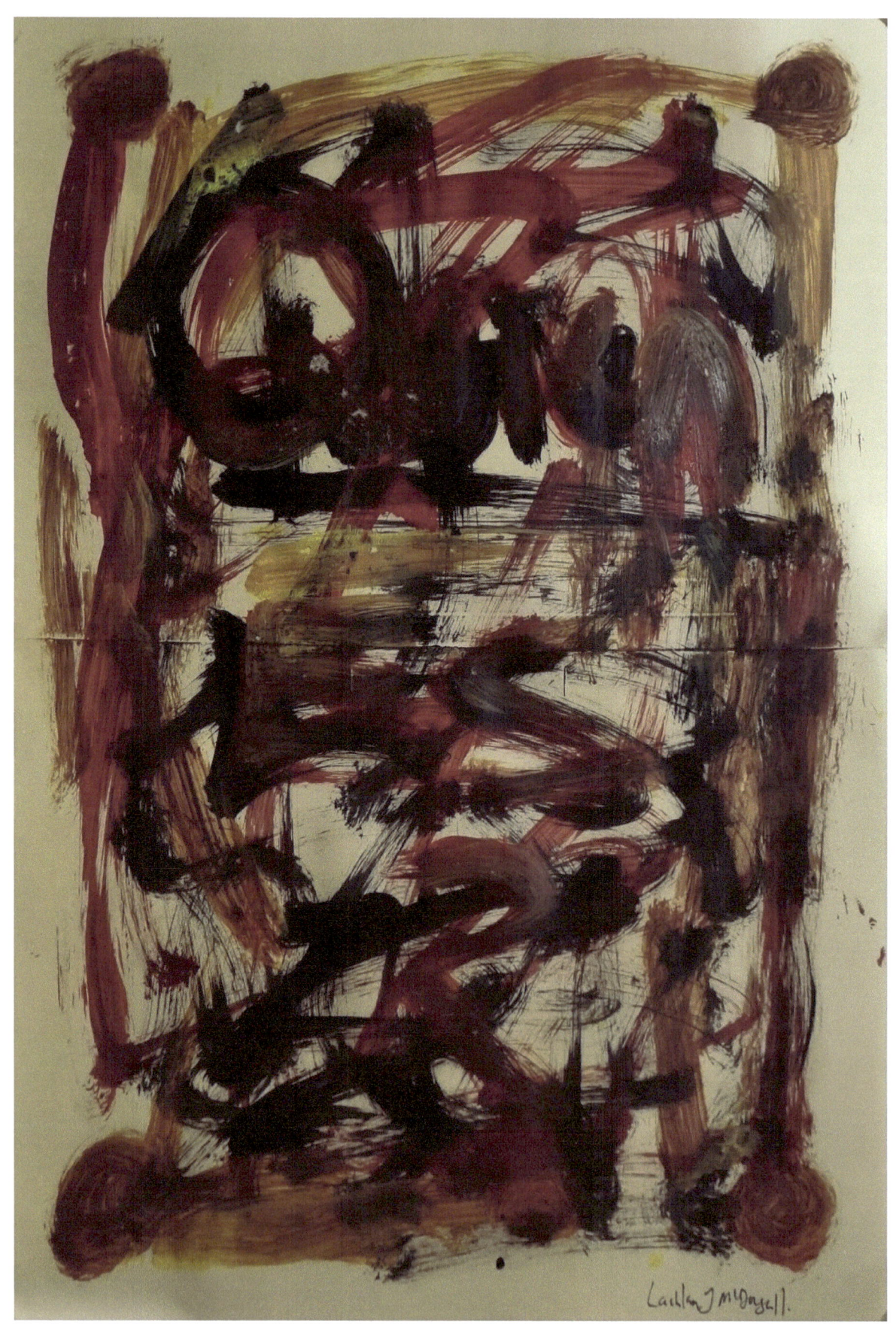

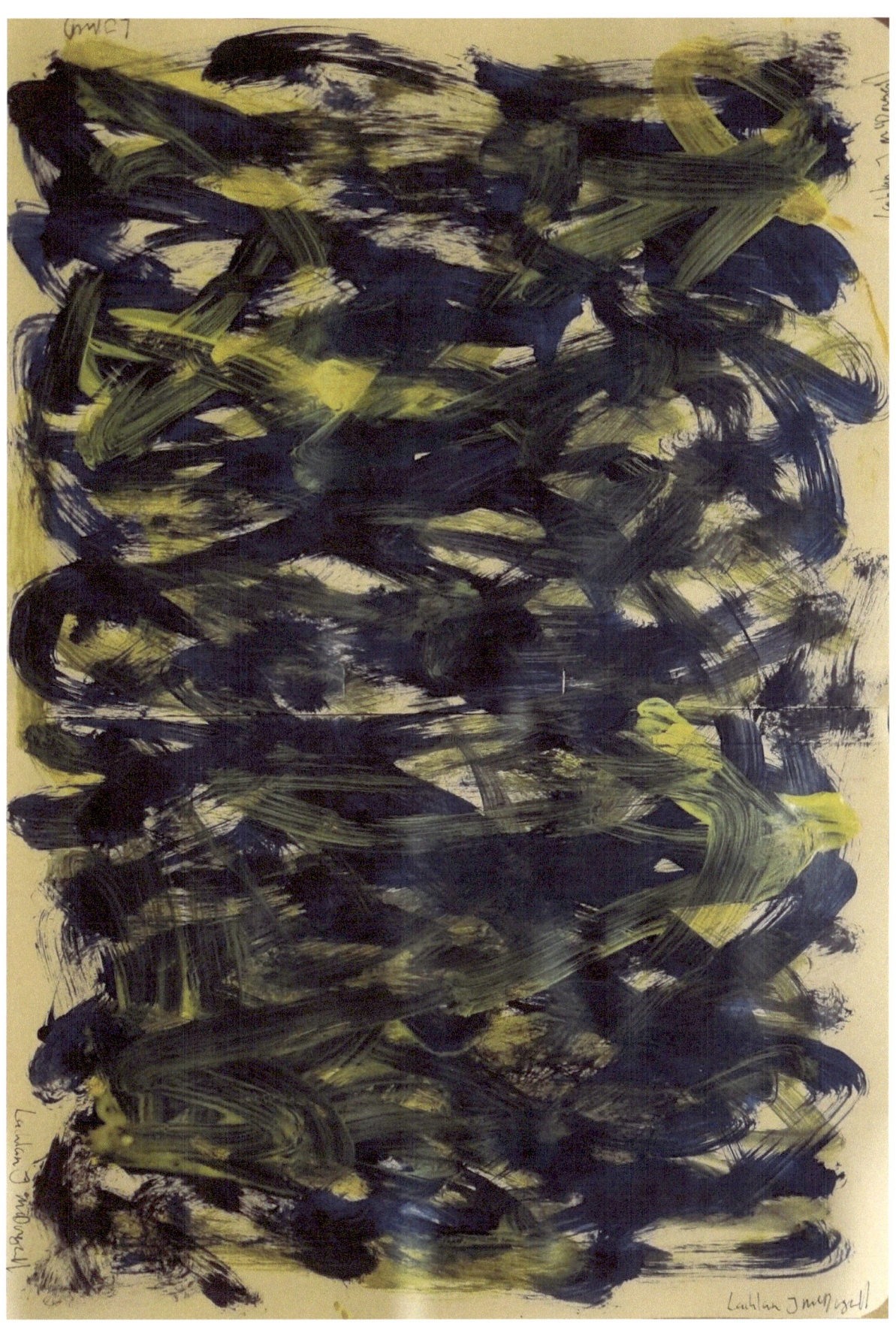

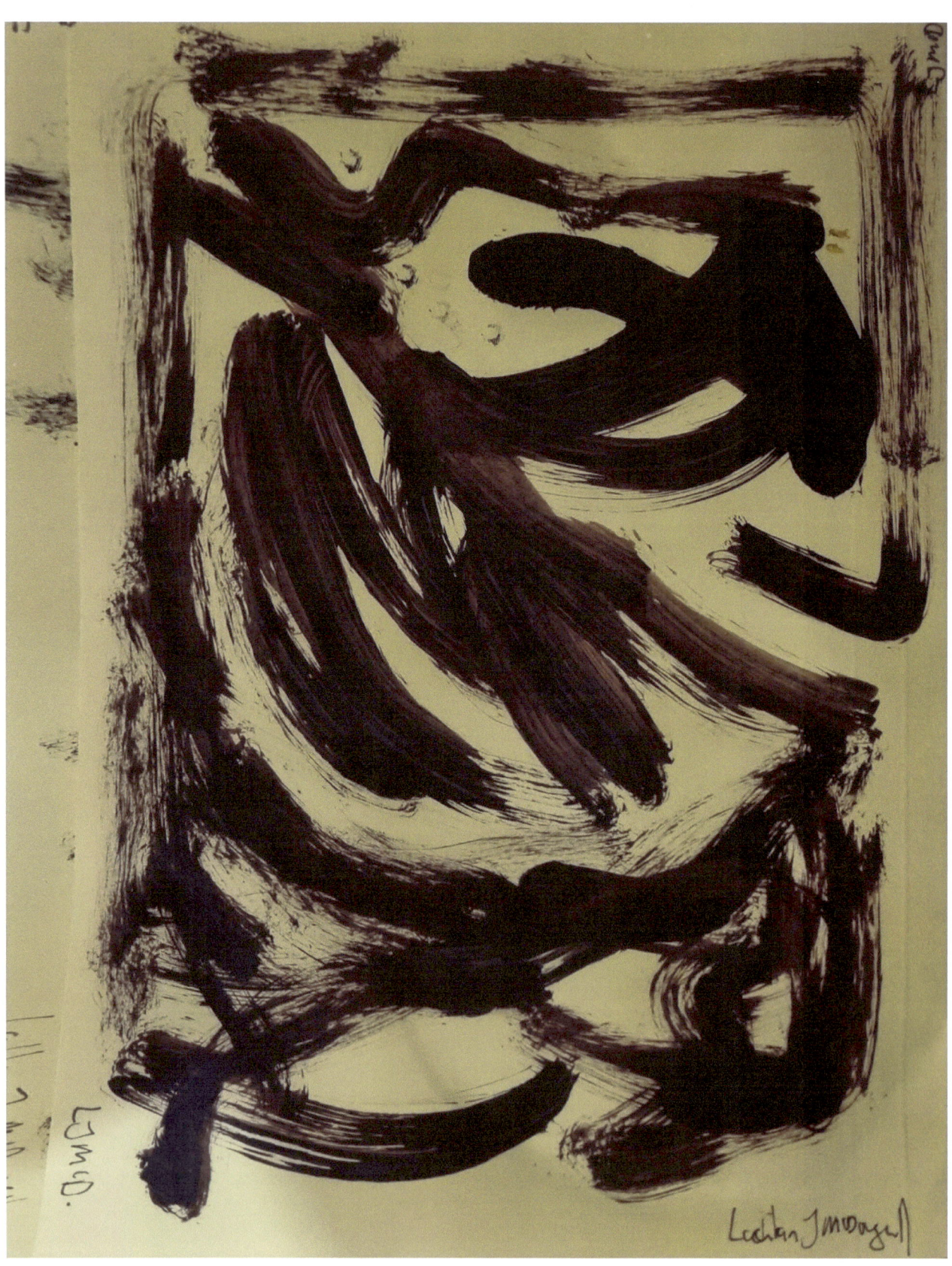

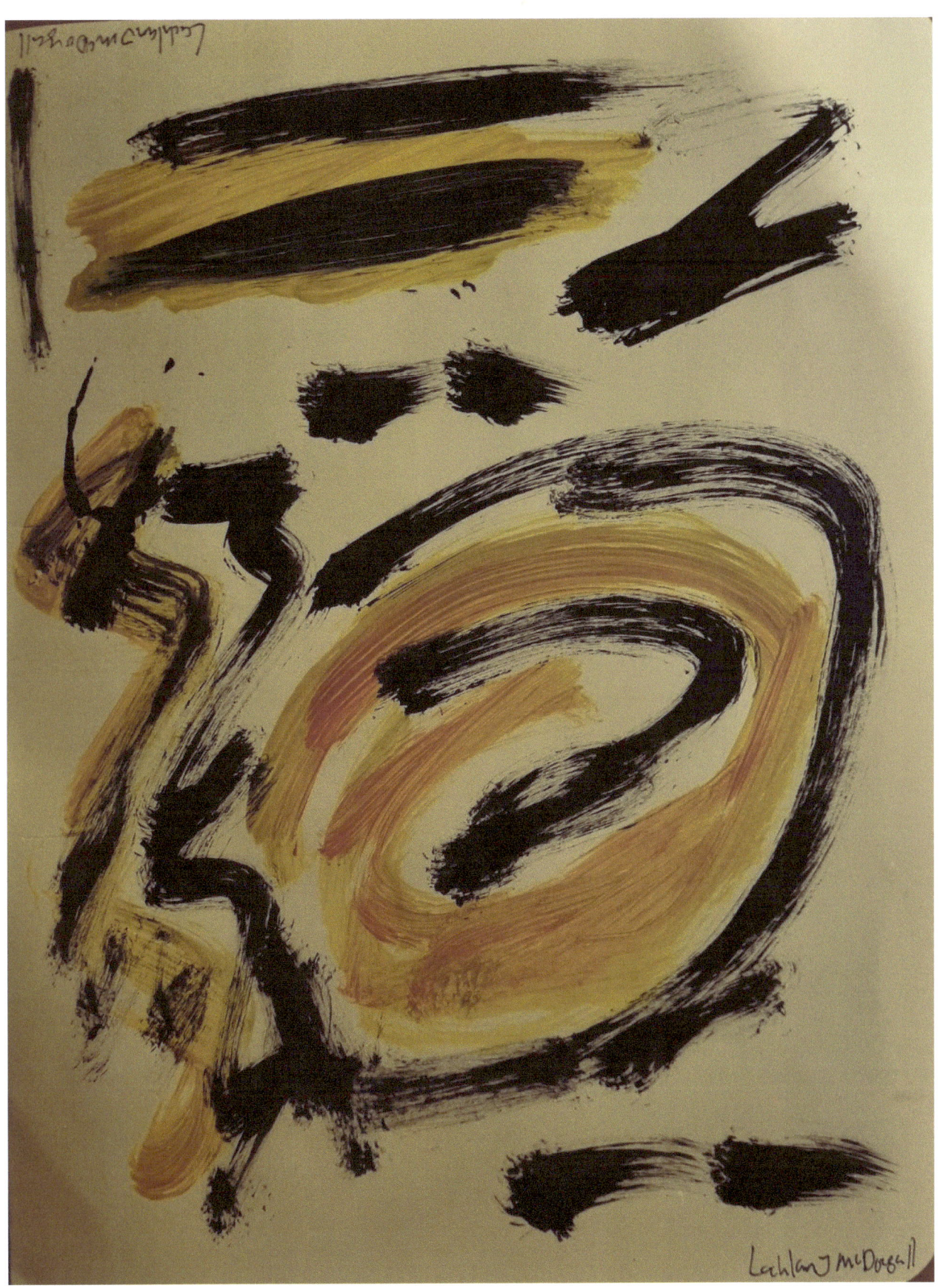

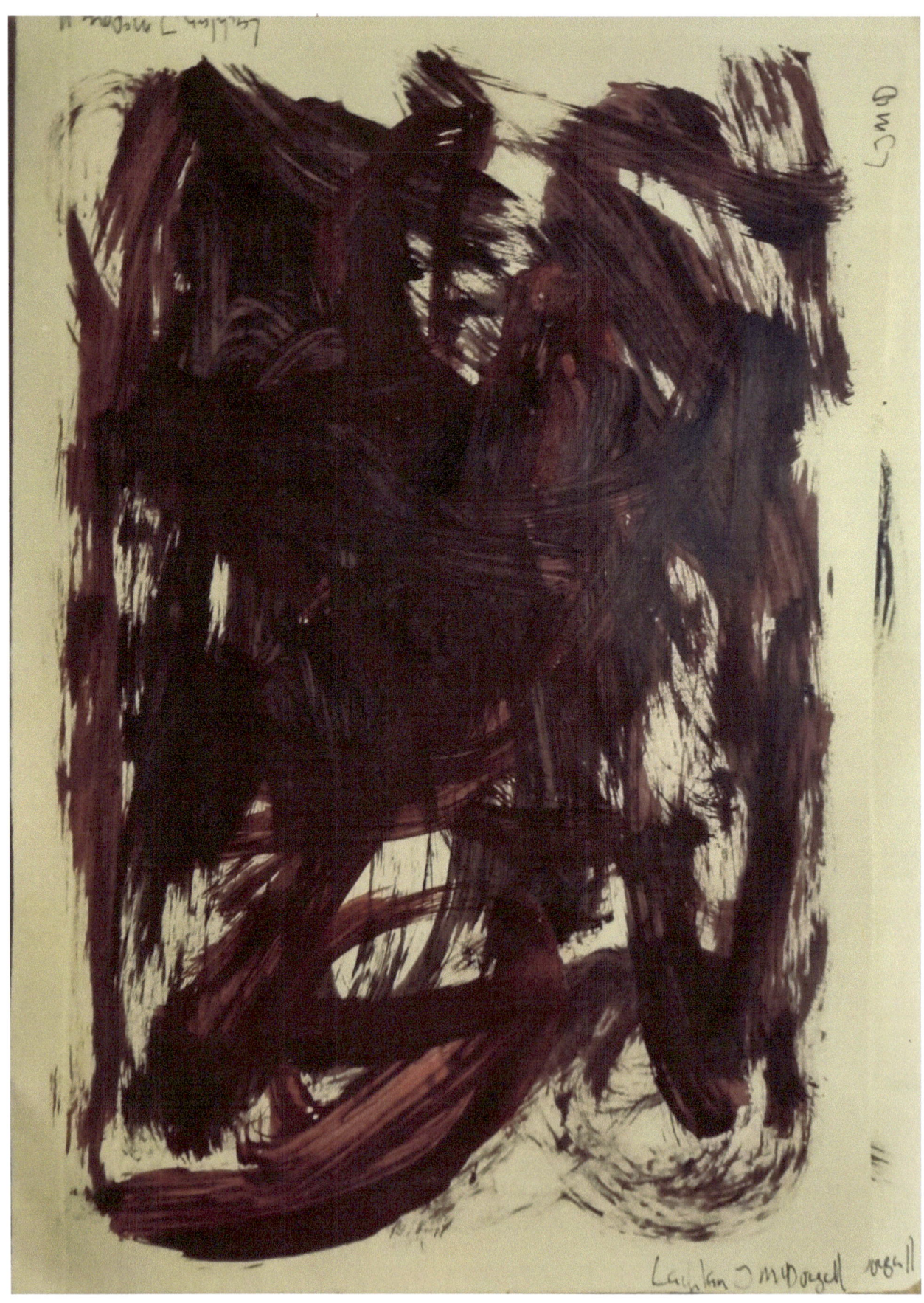

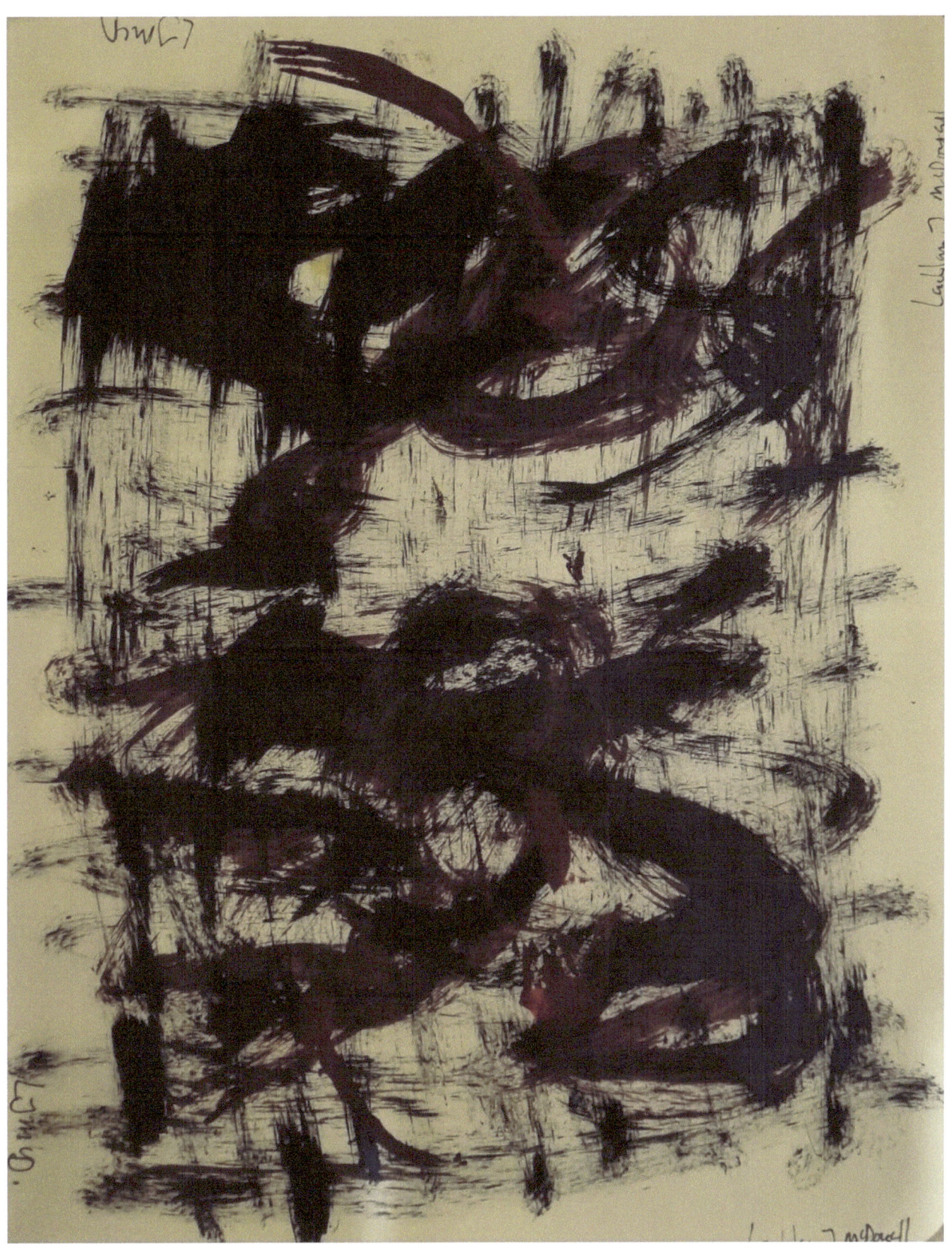

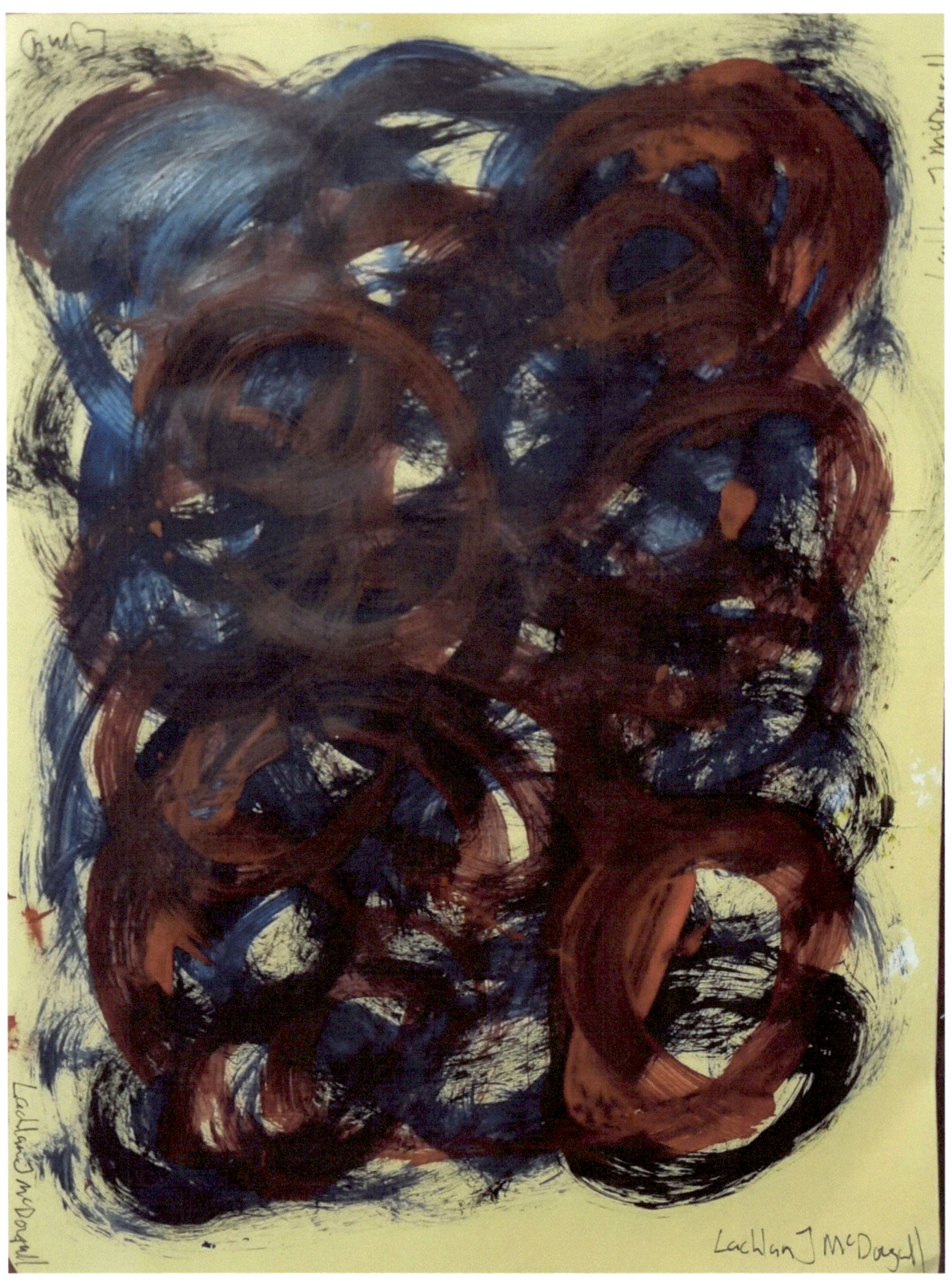

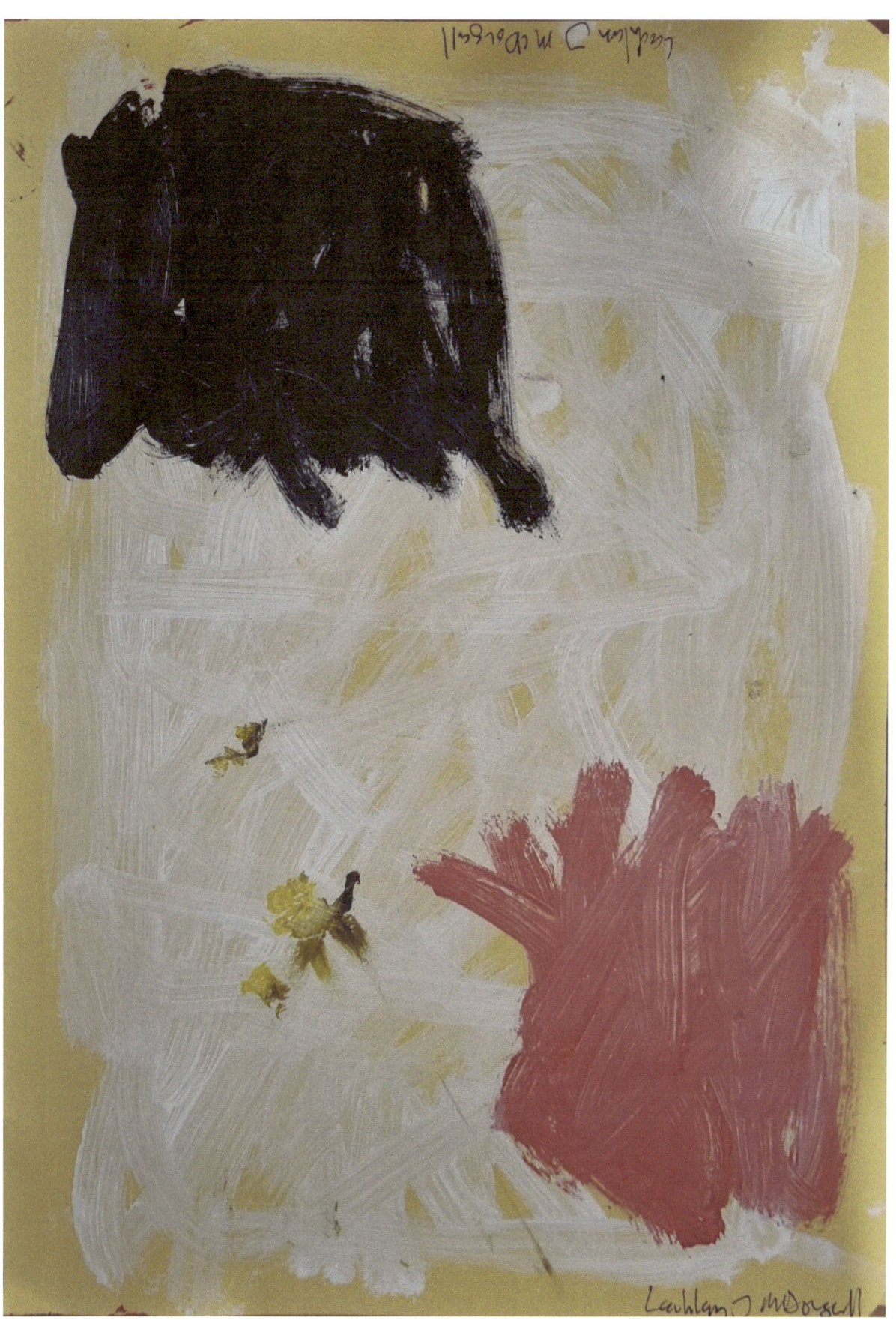

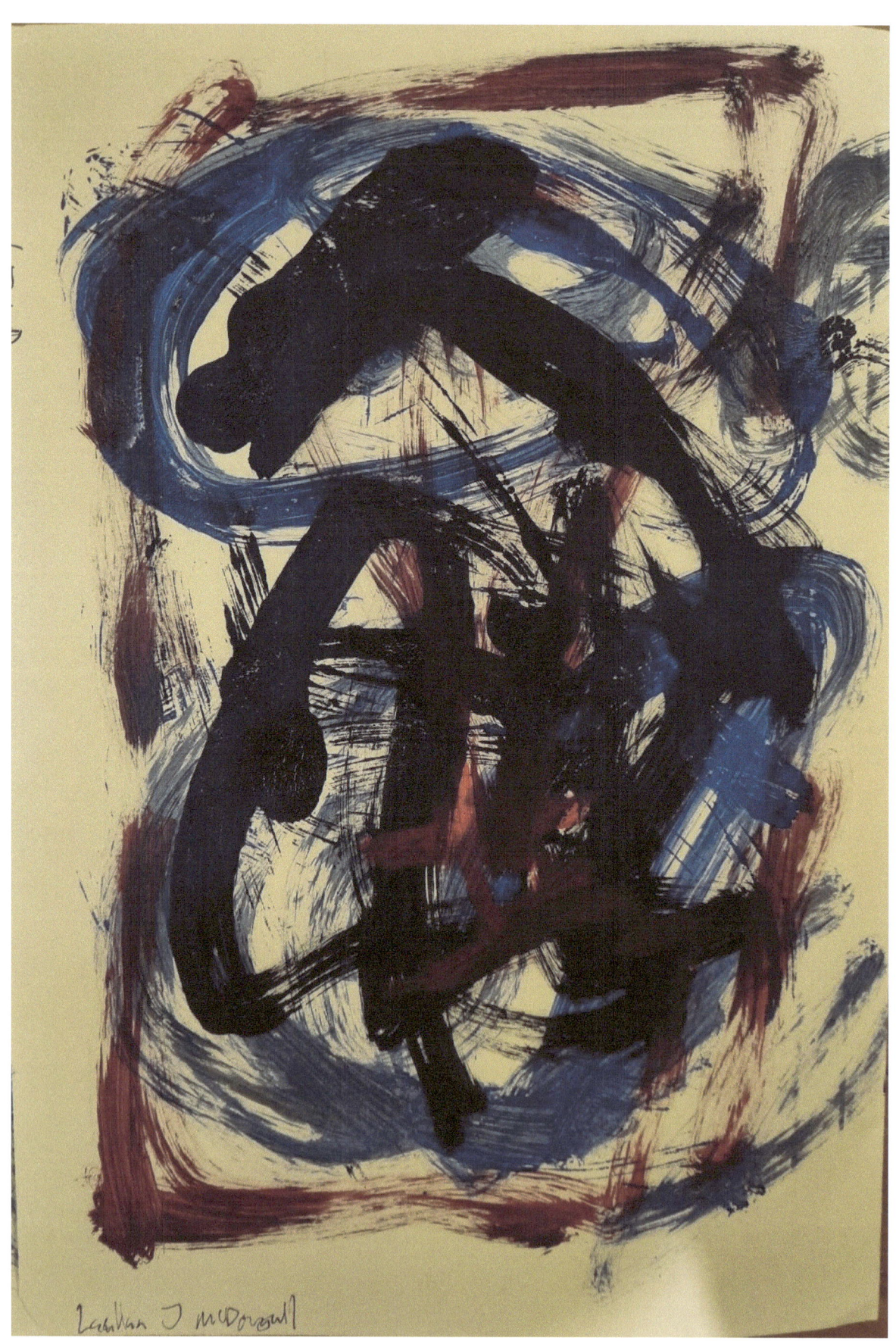

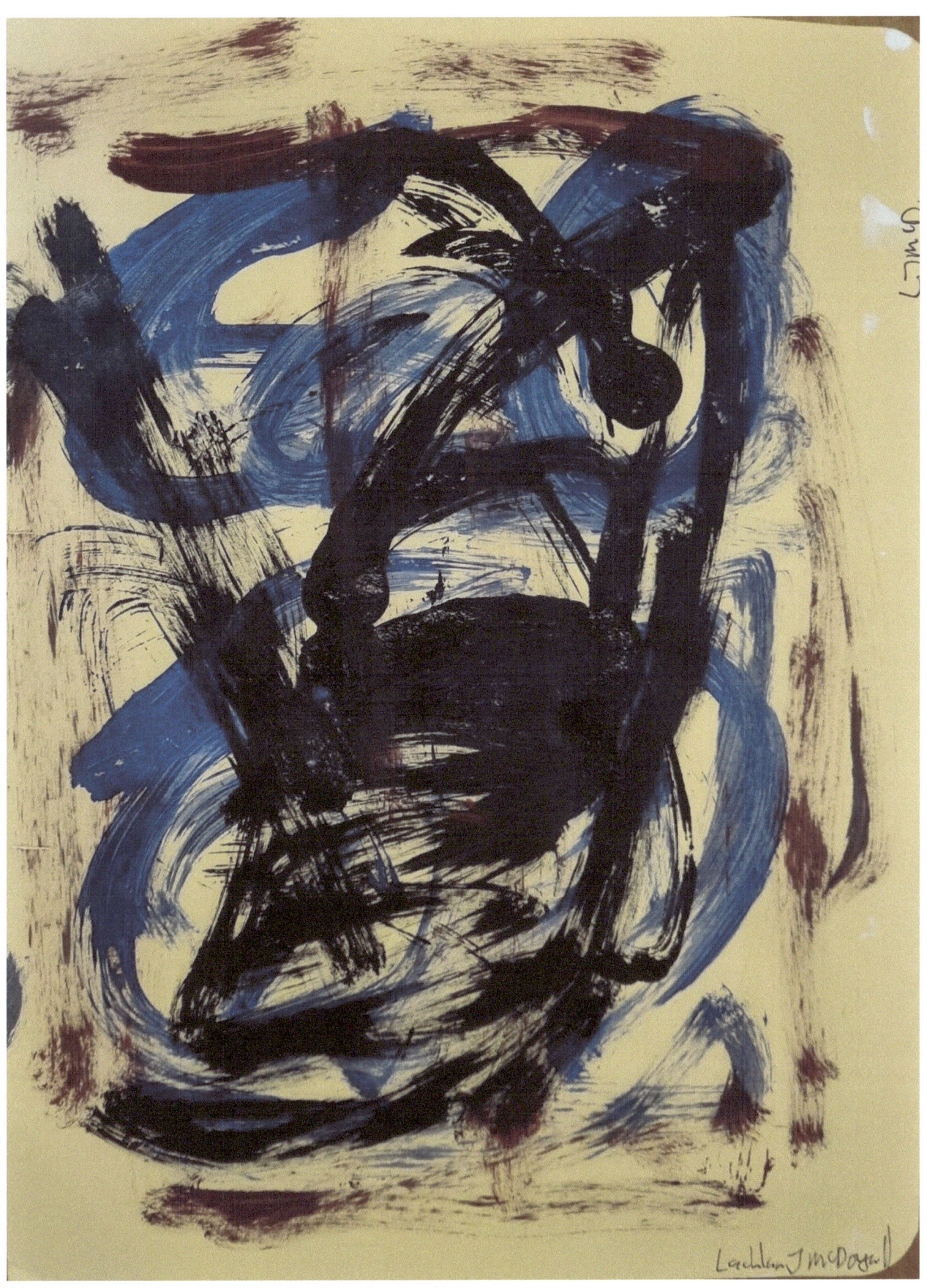

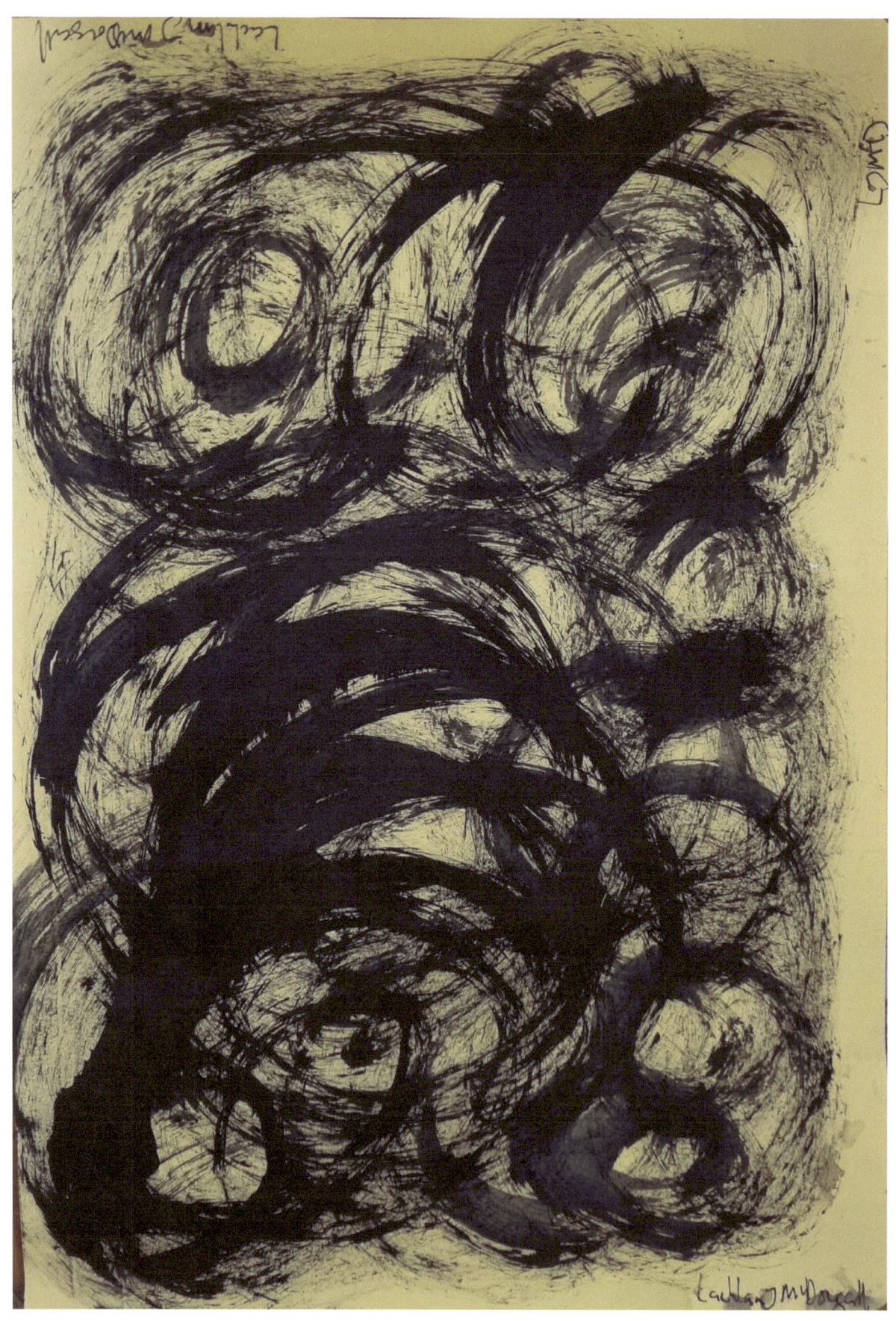

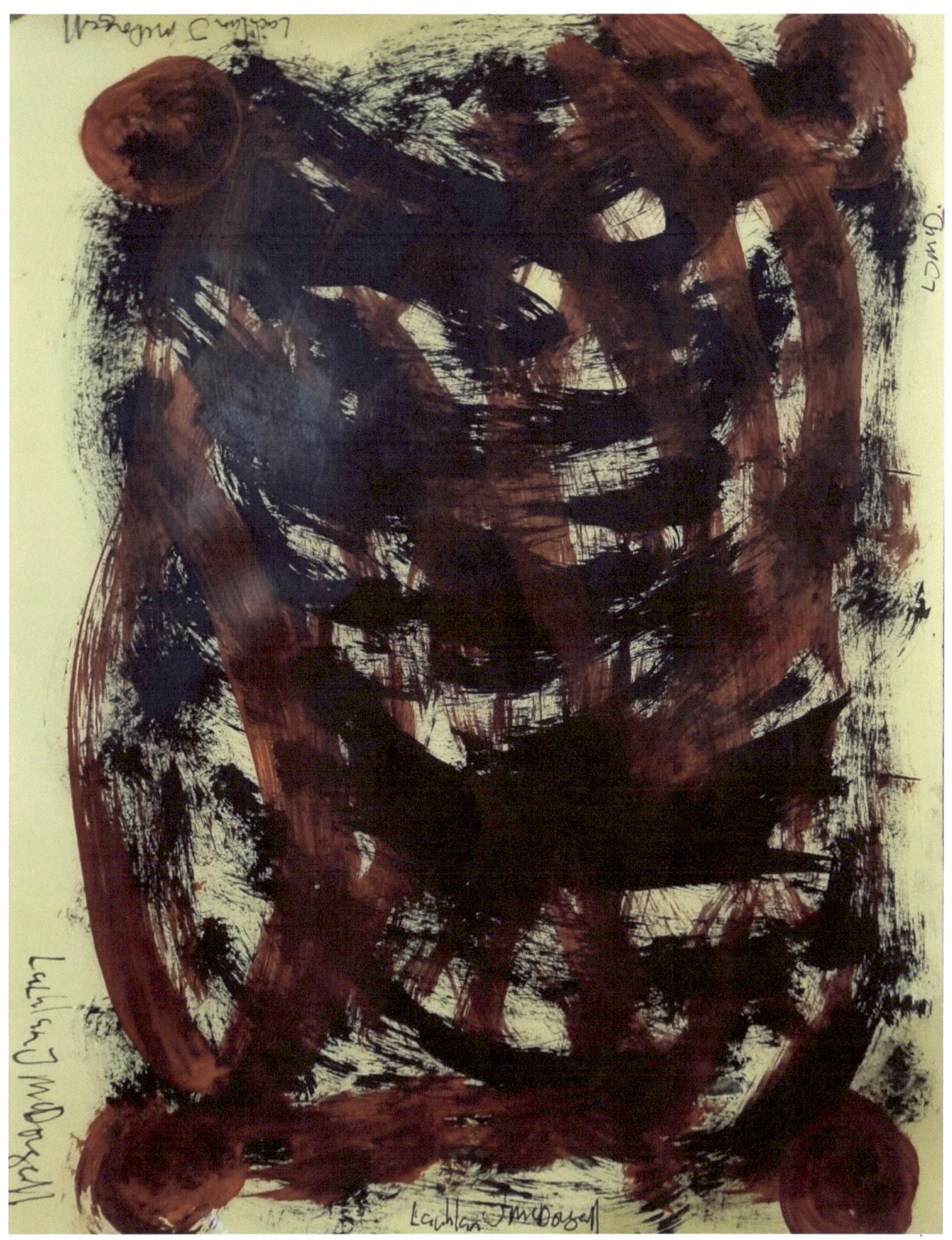

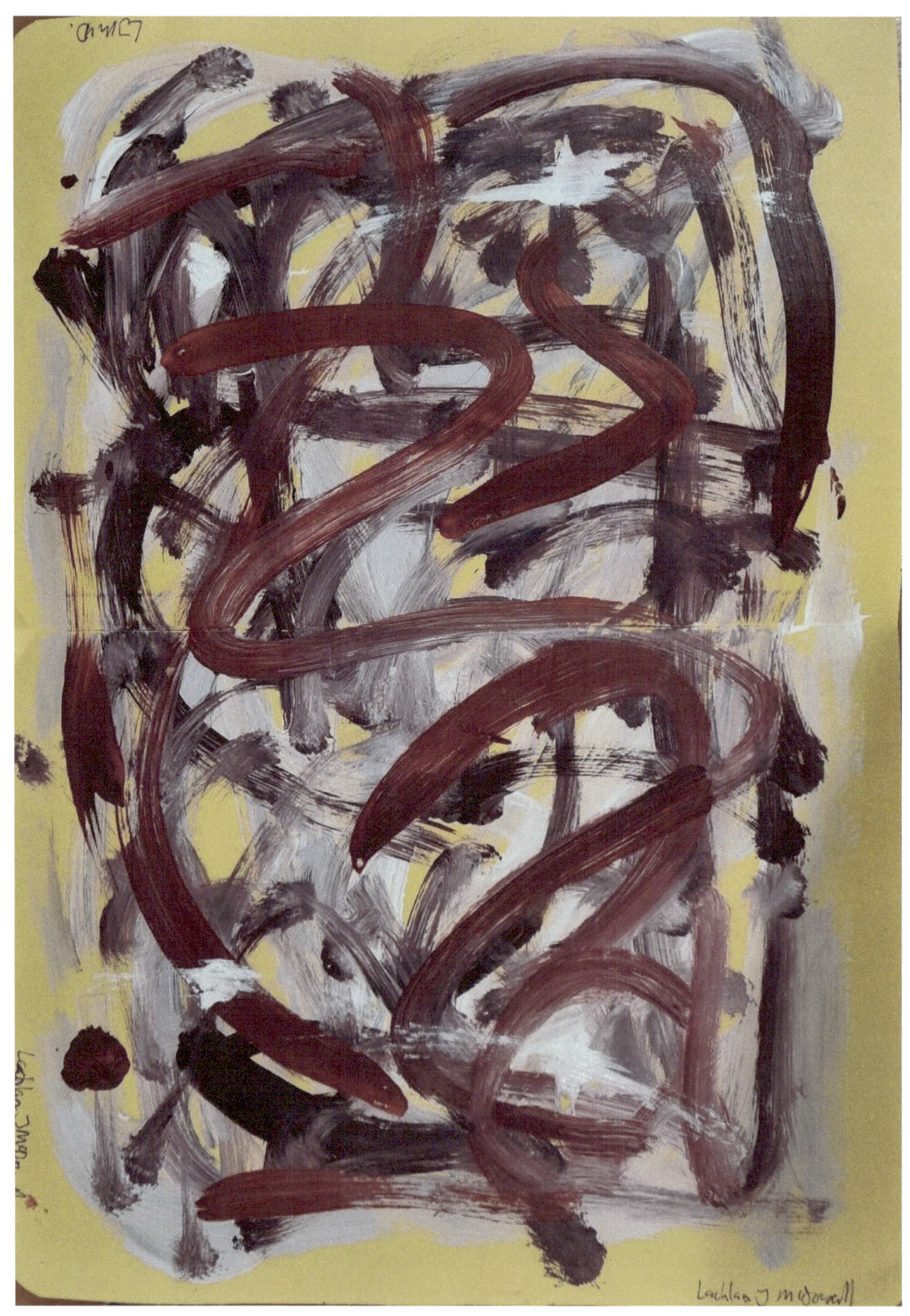

OTHER VISUAL TITLES FROM
LACHLAN J MCDOUGALL:

NOTEBOOK SKETCHES

CATALOGUE OF VISUAL ART 2022

TWELVE PHOTOGRAPHS OF SILENCE

NEGATIVELAND

ALL BOOKS AVAILABLE FROM AMAZON.COM OR EMAILING LACHLAN.MCDOUGALL@GMAIL.COM WITH YOUR ORDER DETAILS

www.ingramcontent.com/pod-product-compliance
Lightning Source LLC
Chambersburg PA
CBHW040432220526
45473CB00004B/1414